HOPE

A COLLECTION OF
OBAMA POSTERS AND PRINTS

Hal Elliott Wert

ZENITH PRESS

First published in 2009 by Zenith Press, an imprint of
MBI Publishing Company, 400 1st Avenue North, Minneapolis,
MN 55401 USA.

Zenith Press titles are also available at discounts in bulk quantity
for industrial or sales-promotional use. For details write to Special
Sales Manager at MBI Publishing Company, 400 1st Avenue North,
Minneapolis, MN 55401 USA.

To find out more about our books, join us online at
www.zenithpress.com.

Editor: Steve Gansen
Jacket Designer: John Barnett/ 4 Eyes Design
Book Designer: Brenda C. Canales

On the cover: A detail from the poster *Grant Park*
by David Springmeyer
Inside the dust jacket: *Hope* by David Choe
Endpaper collages: Billi Kid
On the frontispiece: A detail from the poster *Street*
by Ray Noland
On the title page: *Speaking to US* by Ray Noland

Library of Congress Cataloging-in-Publication Data

Wert, Hal Elliott.
  Hope : a collection of Obama posters and prints / Hal Elliott Wert.
    p. cm.
  ISBN-13: 978-0-7603-3787-5 (hb w/ jkt)
  ISBN-10: 0-7603-3787-X
 1. Obama, Barack—Pictorial works. 2. Presidents—United
States—Election—2008—Pictorial works. 3. Campaign
paraphernalia—United States—History—21st century—Pictorial
works. 4. Presidential candidates—United States—History—21st
century—Pictorial works. 5. Political campaigns—United States—
History—21st century—Pictorial works. 6. Political posters,
American—History—21st century. I. Title.
  E906.W47 2009
  324.973075—dc22
                                                2009013537

Printed in China

For William Ira "Bill" Wert,
brother, friend, veteran, artist, and
bon vivant

Unite US 2008 | Nicholas Rock | 26" x 40"

CONTENTS

Foreword by Ray Noland   9

Introduction   10

The Collection   15

Epilogue   138

Acknowledgments   152

Catalog of Posters and Prints   153

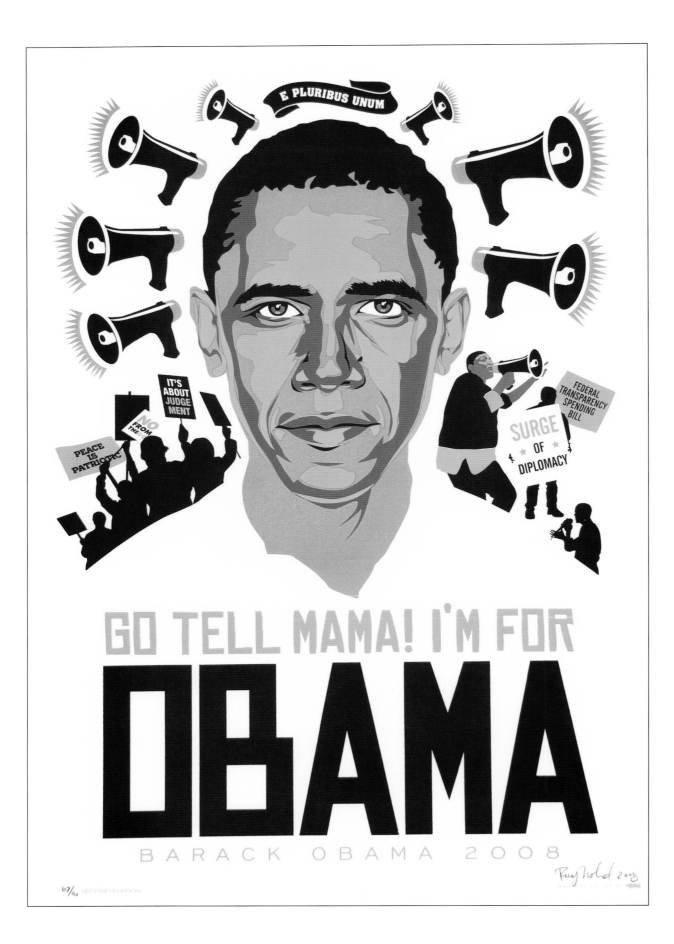

Go Tell Mama! | Ray Noland | 18" x 24"

FOREWORD

WHAT AN INTERESTING JOURNEY this Obama art movement has been! As the creator of Go Tell Mama!, an independent art campaign for Obama, my earliest intention was simply to direct people's attention to this unknown junior senator. He was the textbook underdog in the year leading up to the primary elections, and we were fiercely combating the foregone conclusion that the Clintons were entitled to the Democratic nomination. What developed alongside the grueling campaign trail was a catalog of visual support from every corner of the country—as diverse as our nation itself.

Hal Elliott Wert has been on the hunt, diligently collecting my prints from the earliest days of the movement. Later, I came to realize he was not only collecting my body of work but amassing every morsel of Obama art he came across. Hal's perspective as a historian makes him uniquely qualified to contextualize the story of artists' participation in this seminal moment in American history.

When I met Hal face to face, he told me a story about when he had the rare chance to buy a McCarthy campaign poster for the 1968 election but at the time didn't have the money. Looking back I think he felt a bit of regret that that opportunity passed him by—a mistake not to be made twice. So when the groundswell started to develop, Hal was first in line.

Some will argue this was all a manifestation of the well-oiled campaign machine. But I think the culture that existed beyond the bounds of official messaging and branding took on a powerful life of its own. In fact, creative types were manifesting the idea visually before Obama had even officially announced his candidacy.

Hope: A Collection of Obama Posters and Prints tells the whole story. As an artist I'm really grateful that Hal saw the importance of this work and undertook the mission to document the story from start to finish.

—Ray Noland, Creative Rescue Organization (CRO)

The marquee for the Officially Unofficial exhibition in Chicago, where many of the prints and posters you will see on the following pages were on display from April 1 to May 31, 2009. *Ray Noland*

INTRODUCTION

As the BART train shot into the tunnel on the Oakland side of the bay, riders glimpsed large, black-and-white, eye-catching posters heralding "Barack Obama for President"—*Forward, Cambio, Our Time Has Come*. At bus stops in Philadelphia, riders stared at carefully laid out collages of Obama posters plastered along the shelters. Down in Texas, drivers on the back roads and highways passed rows of posters on telephone poles, reminiscent of the old Burma-Shave marketing gimmick, but with an artist's rendering of Barack's visage and with the Spanish slogan "Si Se Puede." In small towns in Ohio and Indiana, still in the grip of winter, posters peeped out from fogged-up restaurant windows with the message "Hope, Progress, and Change."

Ensconced in the American heartland, the Windy City experienced the first great barrage of Obama posters—artists openly disobeying the restriction "post no bills." At night, a shadowy superhero would cruise along on his skateboard through the dark streets of the city, lugging a backpack crammed with a large roll of posters, wheat paste, and a brush. Initialing his slapper posters like the mark of Zorro, "CRO" sought out every urban nook and cranny to paste up his handiwork. Mornings found downtown Chicago passersby admiring bright-colored posters that sprang up overnight like spring mushrooms, red-and-black posters touting Obama's basketball prowess while proclaiming a sweeping political victory *Coast to Coast*. Often accompanying that Saul Bass–influenced poster was *Street*, with Obama's piercing eyes staring at you from a head surrounded by a nimbus. In various combinations these posters made for attention-grabbing installations. Added to this visual blitz was some black-and-white spray-painted stenciling on the sides of white concrete buildings that portrayed Obama speaking into a microphone plugged into a map of the United States—*Speaking to US*.

Clearly the multitude of posters that spontaneously appeared throughout the country did not originate with the Obama campaign. But then, where *did* they come from? Who made them? It hearkened back to the famous World War II graffiti scrawled 'round the world, "Kilroy Was Here," leaving many Americans preoccupied with guessing who was behind it. The anonymous posters had aroused the public's curiosity and created the desired buzz. The search for this stealth poster-maker was now underway in Chicago, the only clue being the three letters scrawled in the poster's lower right-hand corner. Odds hardly seemed better of discovering CRO than Kilroy.

CRO's admirers, and there were many, did extensive computer searches, and he was eventually outed. CRO (which stands for Creative Rescue Organization) was Ray Noland, a slim and intense African-American designer, printmaker, and native Chicagoan. This is where it all started; this was the pebble that presaged the avalanche of Obama campaign posters that would flood America. Little could Noland have suspected that his lonely midnight ventures into the streets of Chicago on behalf of his candidate would be the birth of a nationwide political art movement. Later, after Obama's victory and after the dust had settled, Noland, sitting with his girlfriend in an east Pilsen café, said, "Can you believe how far this has come?" It really was a long, thrilling roller-coaster ride.

Other artists independently began to produce posters. Shepard Fairey released his retro-design screen print *Vote* in the fall of 2007 and then climbed aboard the Obama movement on January 30, 2008, with the release of *Progress*. On February 15, he released *Hope*, soon to become the iconic poster that would brand the Obama campaign. The pebble had now become a boulder and was picking up speed. Benjamin Kuehn had Obama posters on eBay, the primary and caucus calendar accelerated, and the artist collective Upper Playground in San Francisco weighed in with its first poster *Hope*, by "the Mac," quickly followed by the Date Farmers' *Si Se Puede*. Like CRO in Chicago, guerrilla poster makers appeared in other cities and created a heightened interest in Obama and unwittingly in themselves. In Oakland the phantom poster-paster was revealed to be "Eddie," just plain Eddie, and the most prolific stealth poster maker in Seattle was never identified—mission accomplished.

This group of mostly young, anti-establishment, skateboarder street artists was unique among political art movements in that it was not officially part of the Obama campaign. Rejecting the mantra of their radical predecessors, "turn on, tune in, drop out," these artists chose to drop in, becoming more deeply engaged and aware than ever. Nor were they afraid of capitalizing to help the cause. Money from the sale of limited editions and from fundraising musical and art events produced the cash to buy thousands of cheap offset prints. These posters were then shipped to the early primary states of Texas and Pennsylvania. Importantly, it was not just posters, politics, and rock 'n' roll—been there, done that. Newly implemented agitprop activities used the cutting edge communication technologies that were now integral to the younger generation's identity—e-mail, the cell phone, video cameras, websites, iPods, YouTube, Facebook, MySpace, Twitter, podcasts, webisodes. Nighttime guerilla poster actions were documented, and the videos and pictures were disseminated worldwide by morning. The young artists were the change and the future, and they knew it. Wisely, the Obama campaign knew it too, and counted on it. Being cool, being hip, included being the master of the new technologies. To the outsider artists, Obama was a member of the tribe, "he got it," while most of the other candidates did not. Game on, the art movement was now racing down a hill, getting bigger all the time.

The Obama campaign's recognition of the importance of this outsider hip-hop support and the great poster designs emerging from around the country had an impact on the thinking of insider campaign planners. Aside from Sol Sender, Andy Keene, and Amanda Gentry's Obama logo, the campaign's early posters looked like the same run of boring, big-advertising-firm designs that had come to dominate political campaigns for far too long. In late spring 2008, Obama for America announced a series of fine-art prints called *Artists for Obama*, issued in limited editions as fundraisers. Shepard Fairey's poster, *Change*, was the first in the series and was followed by works from more established artists like Scott Hansen, Antar Dayal, Rafael Lopez, Robert Indiana, Lance Wyman,

A baby girl admires a section of the large collage that greets visitors to the Officially Unofficial exhibition at the Chicago Tourism Center. *Cara Rieckenberg*

Jonathan Hoefler, Gui Borchert, and Lou Stovall. The campaign finished the series with a second Shepard Fairey poster.

By that time Fairey had become the darling of the Obama camp, the outsider/insider, and a household name throughout the country. His various Obama images adorned not just posters but flyers, yard signs, billboards, bumper stickers, brochures, rack cards, T-shirts, sweatshirts, coffee mugs, earrings, bracelets, pendants, and a wonderful series of large oval stickers and sheets with a dozen stickers. Stickers were cool, stickers were in, and Obama stickers were everywhere. The Obama campaign had to appeal graphically to very different constituencies, and it was quite satisfied with the "parallel universe" arrangement of two independent campaign efforts that walked the line differently but in pursuit of the common goal of electing Obama.

As both the Obama and outsider campaigns gained momentum, many established artists, those who could not be described as guerrilla skateboarder street artists, began to produce limited-edition, signed prints, donating all or part of the earnings to the Obama campaign. This group was also extraordinarily eclectic, ranging from gig-poster artists like Emek Golan, Justin Hampton, Leia Bell, Wes Winship, Kristen Thiele, Robert C. Lee, and Zak Kaplan to fine printmakers and designers like Dee Adams, Deroy Peraza, Lou Stovall, Tom Slaughter, Rafael Lopez, Tim Hinton, Anthony Armstrong, and Paula

Scher and Michael Beirut at Pentagram. The poster movement had international input as well. Emmanuelle Fevre designed three Obama posters for the art show Obama in Paris, held at Dorothy's Gallery. The famous Austrian illustrator Franke submitted a poster entitled *Hope* to the Manifest Hope art contest in Denver and was one of five finalists. Letterpress artist Kishore Nallan in Chennai, India, also weighed in with a typeface Obama portrait. Beautiful dyed cloth images turned up in the markets of Kenya, Tanzania, and South Africa, and in Iraq and Afghanistan his image was woven into hand-dyed rugs. Art for Obama went global.

Nearly all of the posters appearing in this book come from my own personal collection. The range of posters in terms of style varies greatly, as does the experience of the poster makers. Some posters were created by people making first-time ventures into screen prints or giclée prints; others were made by associates in big, established design agencies; and still others are by street artists or well-known American artists like Robert Indiana. The diverse choice of posters for this book honestly reflects the eclectic nature of the outpouring of posters for Obama. I hope you enjoy viewing the eye-popping artwork featured in this book as much as I have enjoyed collecting it.

—Hal Elliott Wert

This collage by Brooklyn street artist Billi Kid celebrates the artwork of many fellow Obama supporters. *Courtesy Billi Kid*

THE COLLECTION

Obama | "Eddie" | 24½" x 36"

Brooklyn for Barack | Jessica Hische | 17" x 11"

Andrew Bird+Dianogah | Kathleen Judge | 20¼" x 30"

Yes We Can | Tom Slaughter | 18" x 30"

New Era | "Eddie" | 25" x 32"

East LA Portrait | Nick Toga | 12½" x 19"

Get It Straight, Obama in '08 | Lashun Tines | 18½" x 24½"

I Want You to Caucus | Official Obama Campaign | 24" x 36"

Obama Is Money | Julian Norman | 24" x 36"

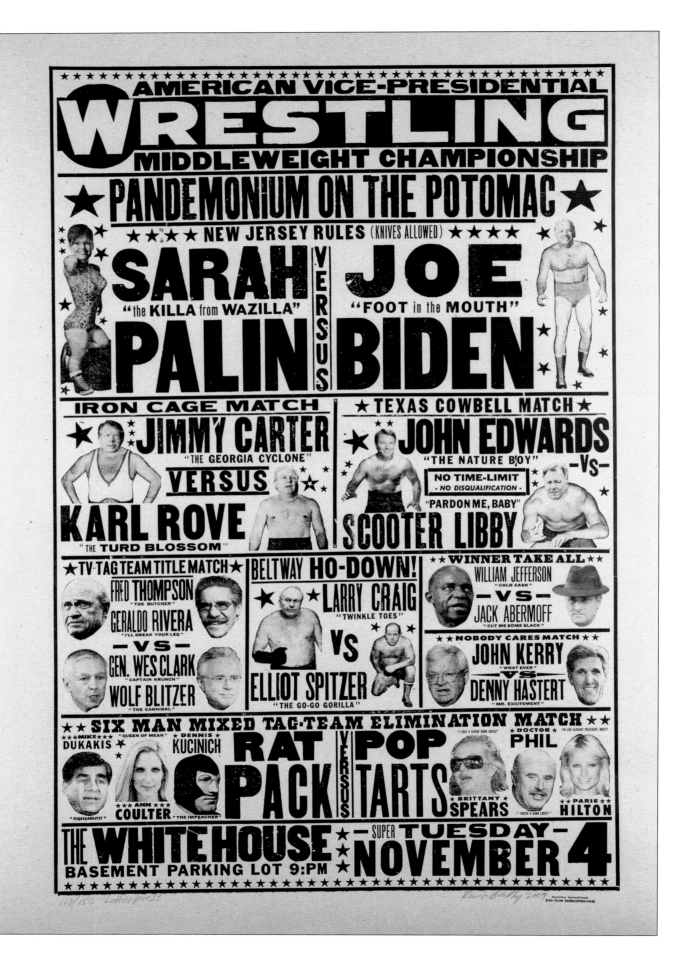

American Vice-Presidential Wrestling Middleweight Championship | Kevin Bradley | 30" x 42½"

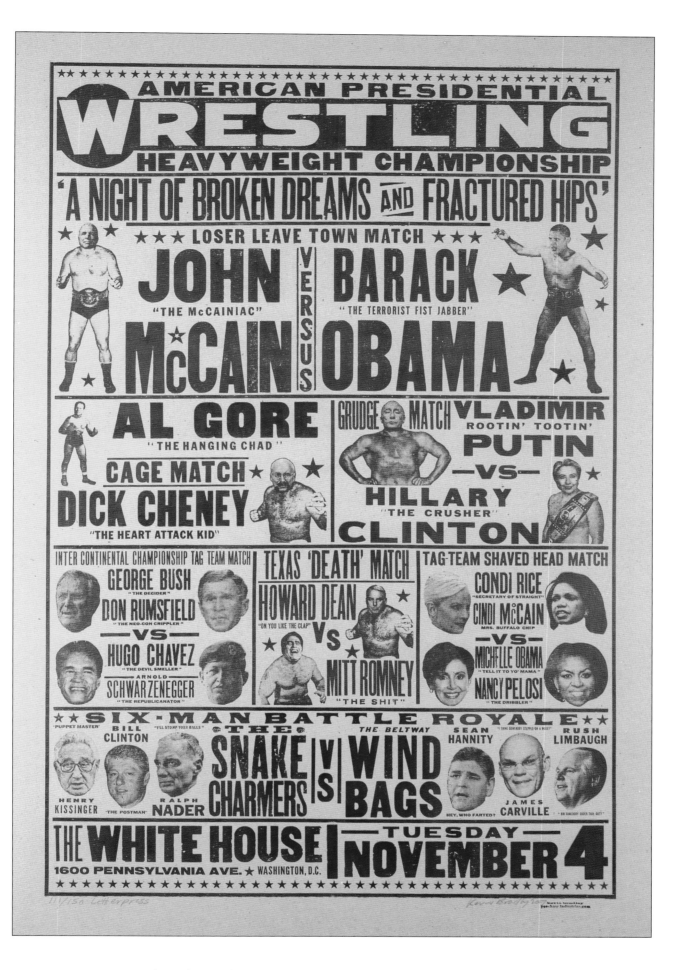

American Presidential Wrestling Heavyweight Championship | Kevin Bradley | 30" x 42½"

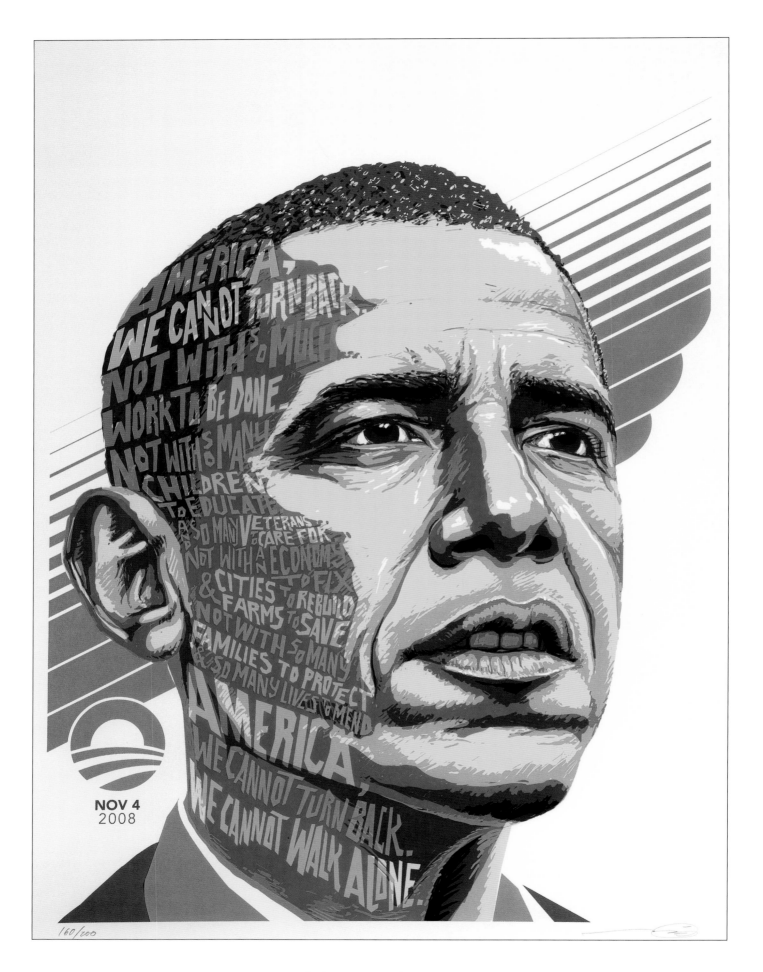

Untitled | Wes Winship | 18" x 24"

PRESIDENT BARACK OBAMA

STAND WITH ME

93/800

President Barack Obama, Stand with Me | Guy Juke | 16¾" x 13"

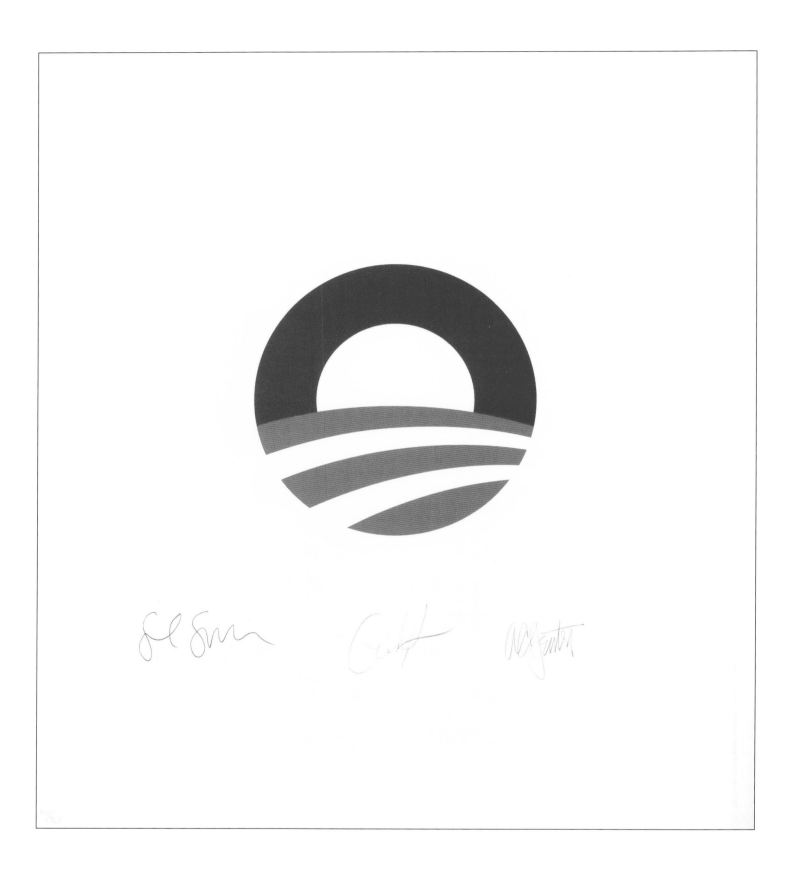

Obama Logo | Sol Sender, Andy Keene, and Amanda Gentry | 18" x 20"

CHANGE

#44

WE CAN BELIEVE IN

13/480

Dayal 08

CHANGE WE CAN BELIEVE IN ANTAR DAYAL www.dayalstudio.com

Change We Can Believe In | Antar Dayal | 28" x 38"

"Color in the Mind's Eye"

827/1500 David Macaluso 9-27-2008

Color in the Mind's Eye | David Macaluso | 20" x 16"

Vote for Change (Michelle Obama) | Official Obama Campaign | 11" x 17"

Democratic Convention 2008 | T. R. Red Corn | 16" x 25"

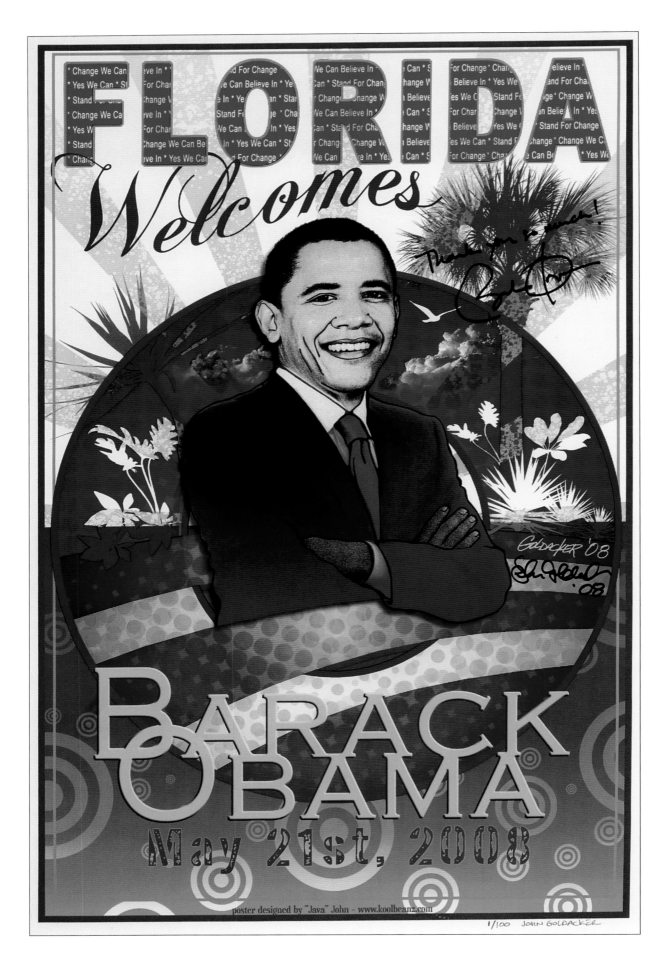

Florida | "Java John" Goldacker | 11¼" x 17"

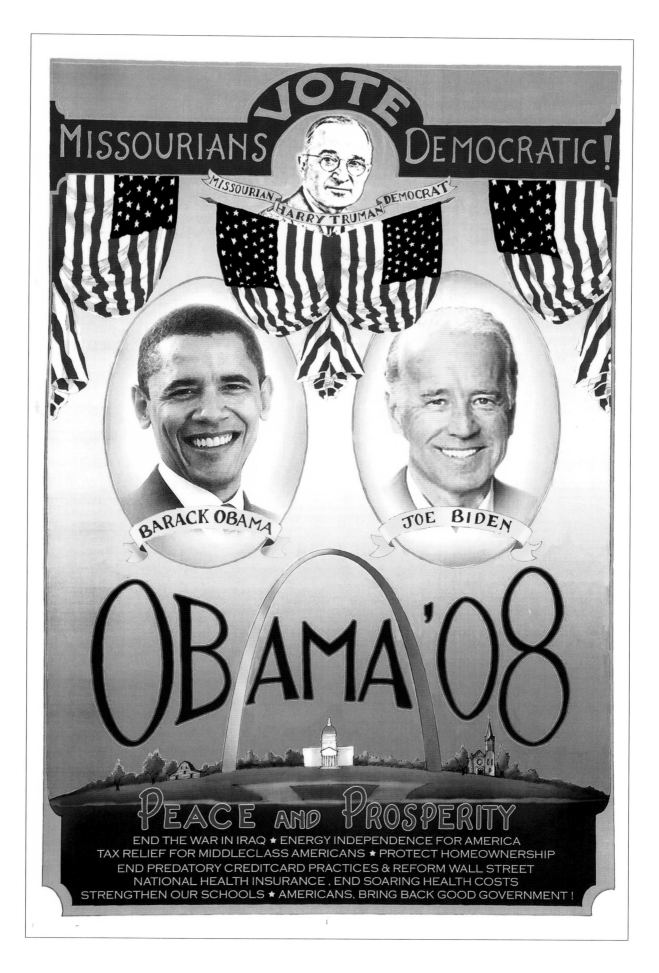

Missouri Democrats for Obama / Biden | Unknown artist | 11" x 17"

Officially Unofficial | Ray Noland | 22½" x 29"

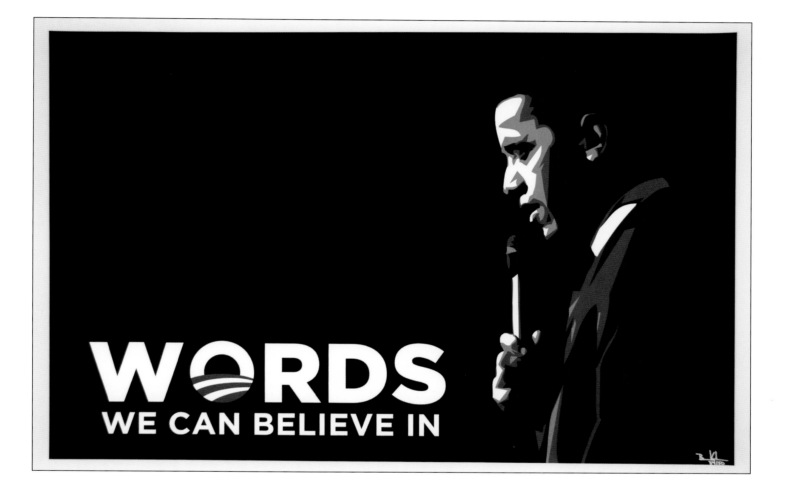

Words We Can Believe In | Benjamin Kuehn | 36" x 24"

Go Tell Mama! (Show) | Ray Noland | 24" x 36"

This Is Our Moment, This Is Our Time | "Eddie" | 36" x 24"

Arcade Fire / Superchunk
Wes Winship | 19" x 25"

Arcade Fire / Superchunk
Kristen Thiele | 19" x 25"

Vote for Change Rally / Bruce Springsteen
Official Obama Campaign | 6" x 8½"

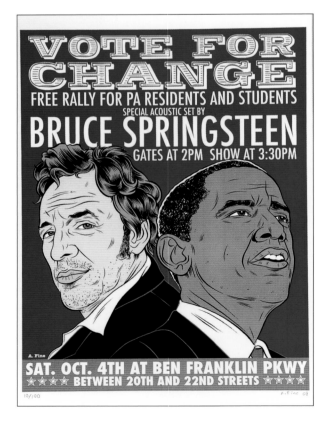

Bruce Springsteen | Alex Fine | 11" x 17"

Grateful Dead | Curt Walters | 10½" x 16⅛"

Abraham Obama | Ron English | Each 23" x 40"

The Hopeful Hearts Club | Michael Cuffe | 11" x 17"

Rock the Vote | Shepard Fairey | 18" x 24"

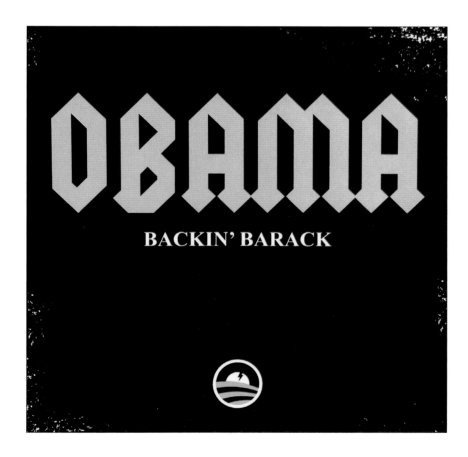

Backin' Barack | Jeffrey Everett | 19" x 19"

Change | Shepard Fairey | 24¾" x 39¼"

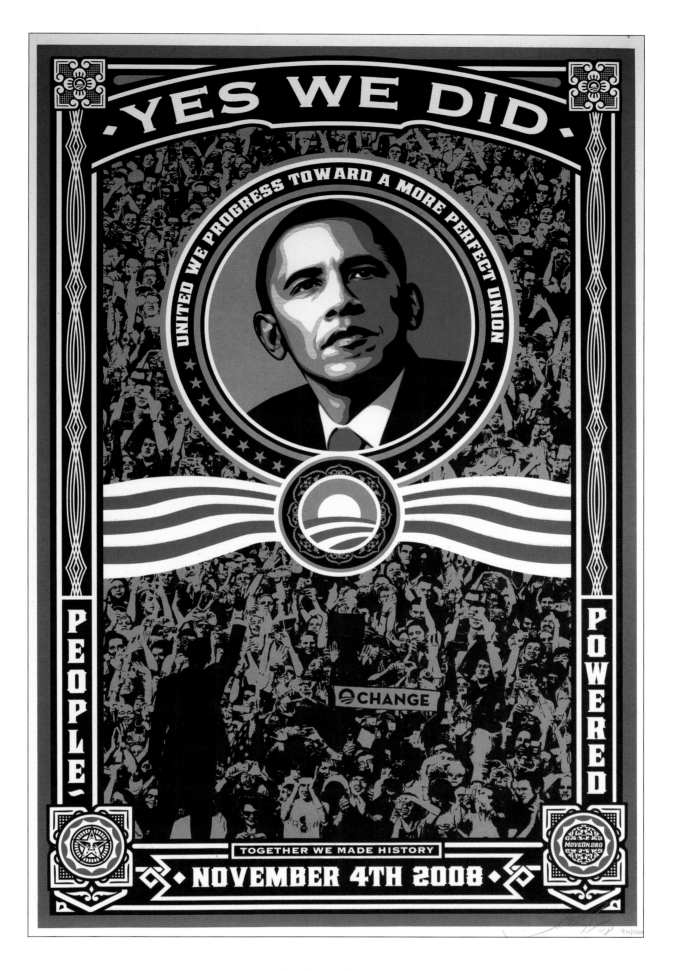

Yes We Did | Shepard Fairey | 24" x 36"

Democracy=Change | Pablo Serrano | 11" x 17"

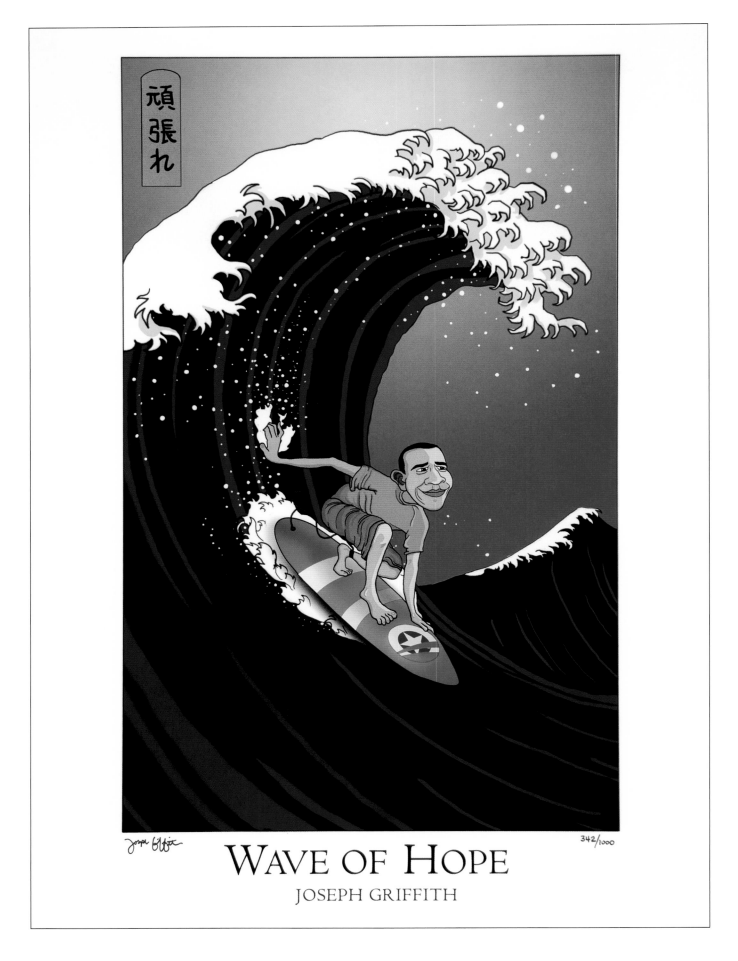

WAVE OF HOPE
JOSEPH GRIFFITH

342/1000

Wave of Hope | Joseph Griffith | 11" x 17"

NOVEMBER 4, 2008

Today is a Big Day | Patrick Moberg | 11" x 8½"

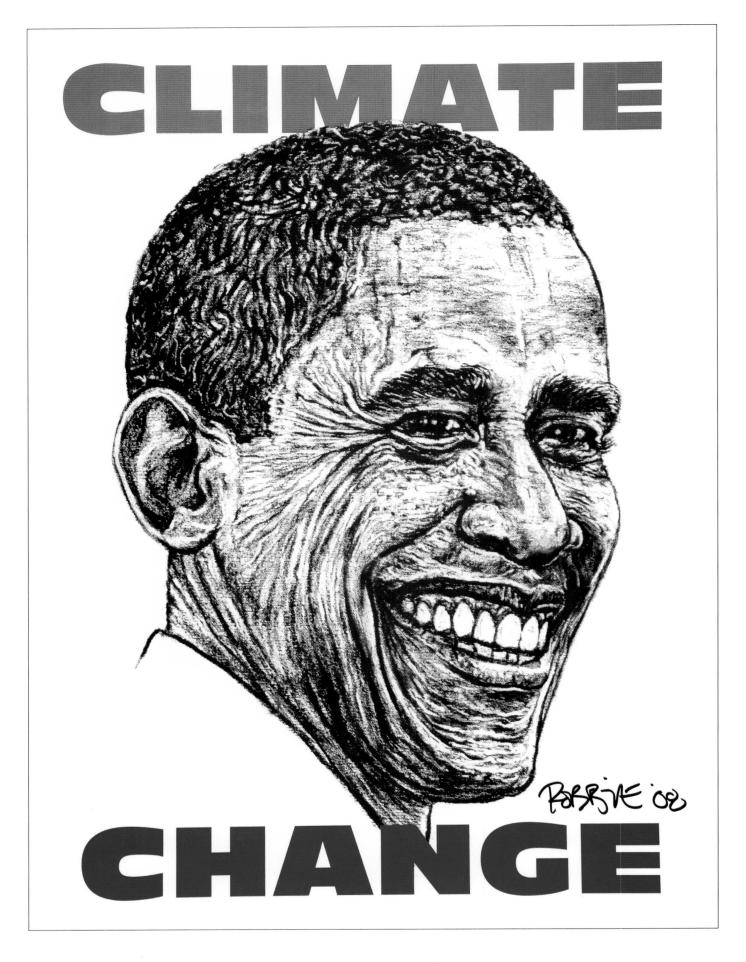

Climate Change | Robbie Conal | 18" x 24"

Yes, Please | Felix Jackson | 18" x 24"

Progress | Scott Hansen | 24¾" x 39"

Barock Easton Registration Drive | Zak Kaplan | 14½" x 20½"

Obama: Yes We Can | Antar Dayal | 28″ x 35¾″

"OBAMA"   DUSTIN PARKER

Hope, Freedom, Change, Progress | Dustin Parker | 20" x 16"

YES, WE CAN

BARACK HUSSEIN OBAMA
44TH AMERICAN PRESIDENT

Yes We Can | Kishore Nallan | 14" x 20"

Allman Brothers Band / Deadheads for Obama | Branden Otto | 14" x 25½"

Superman Obama | "Mr. Brainwash" | 29¼" x 41½"

Obama, President, United States of America | Paul Friedrich | 12" x 18"

We Need Hope / We Need Peace / We Need Change | Mason Fetzer | Each 20" x 29¾"
We One | Mason Fetzer | 11" x 17"

First: Barack Obama | Ray Noland | 18" x 24"

First: Michelle Obama | Ray Noland | 18" x 24"

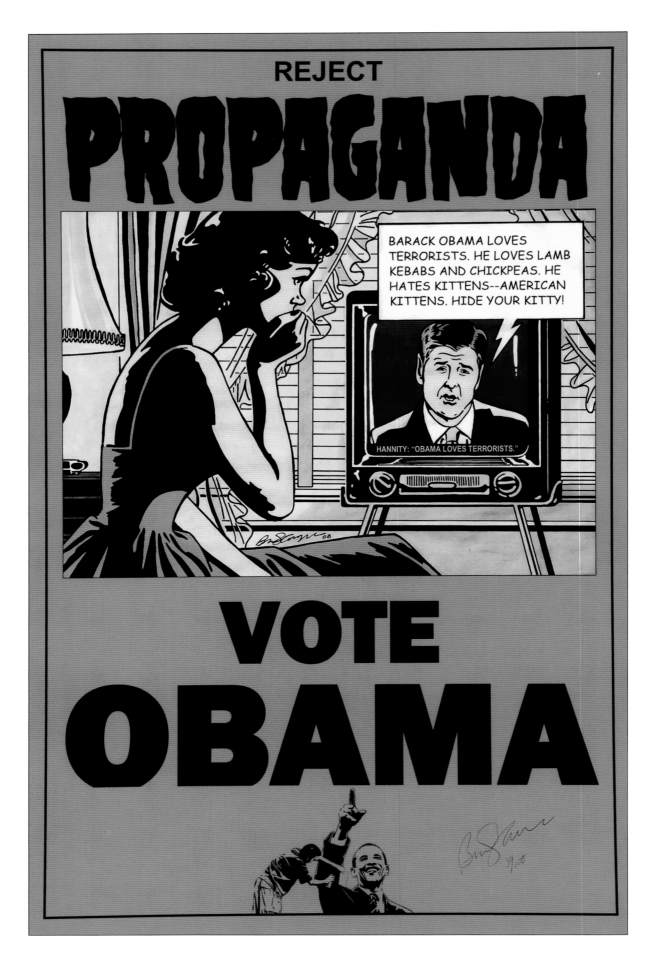

Reject Propaganda | Brian Campbell | 11" x 17"

33/120   "Barack"   Leia Bell 2008

Barack | Leia Bell | 12" x 17"

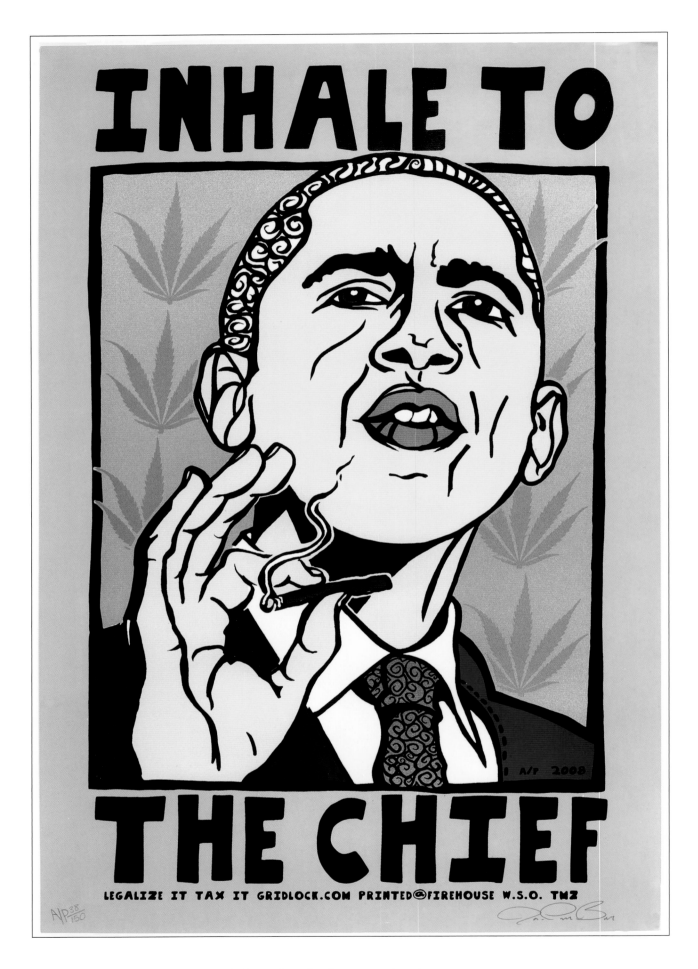

Inhale to the Chief | Jon-Paul Bail | 18" x 24"

WE WANT
CHANGE

20/50

We Want Change | "Mear One" | 18" x 24"

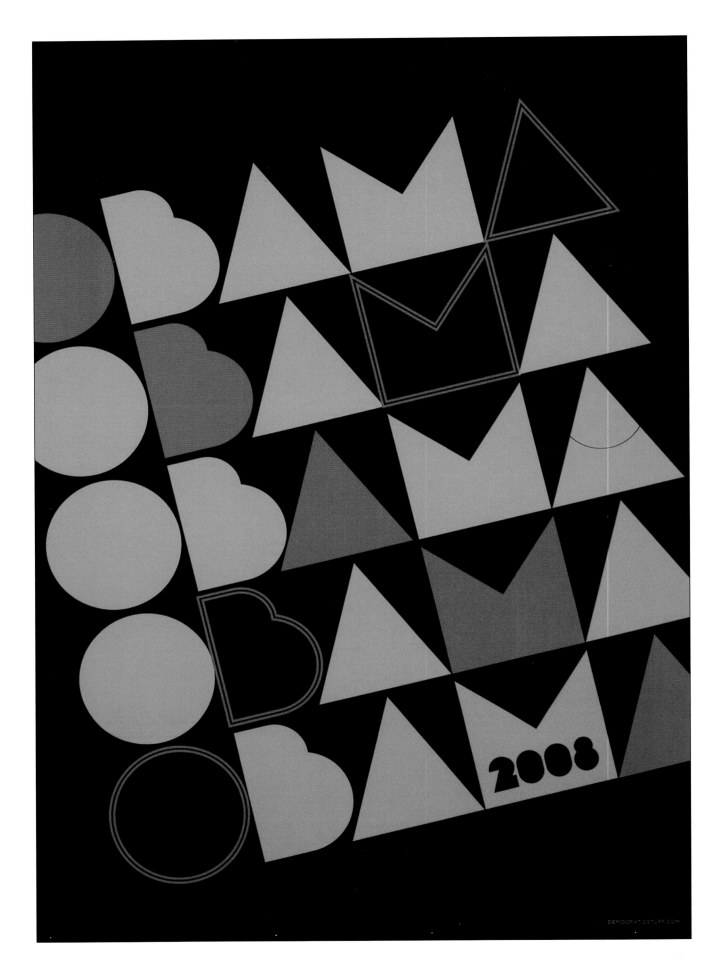

Obama Arcade Lettering | Russell Baltes | 20" x 28"

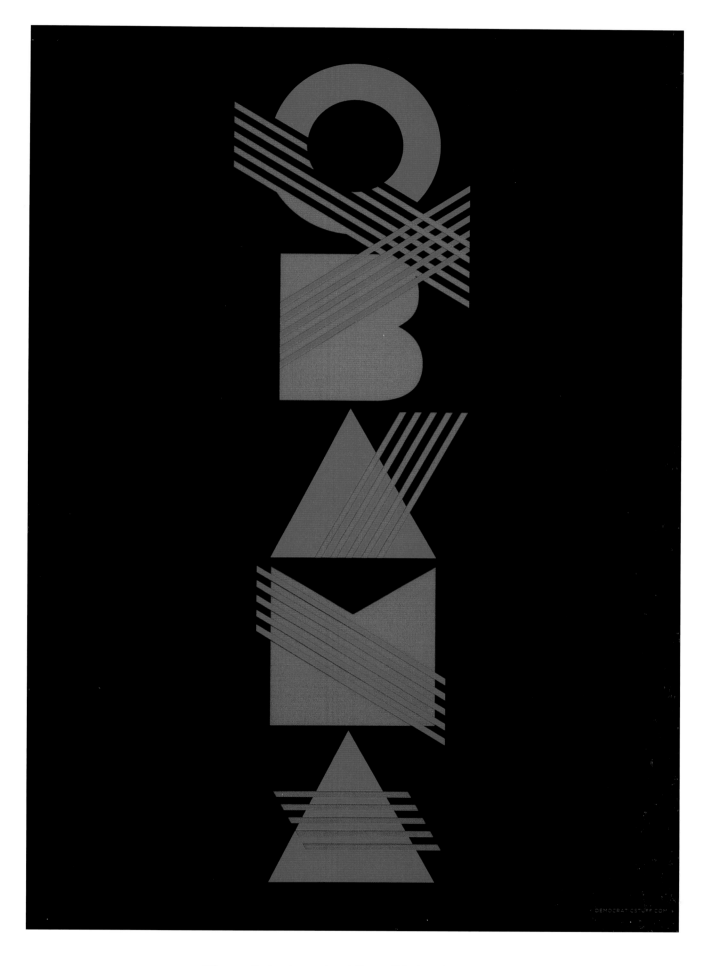

Obama Retro Lettering | Russell Baltes | 20" x 28"

(top left) **Believe** | "Mags" | 11" x 14"

(top right) **The Dream** | Ray Noland | 16½" x 23"

(bottom left) **Obama** | Jason Krekel | 12½" x 19"

(bottom right) **Obama '08** | Unknown artist | 10½" x 14¼"

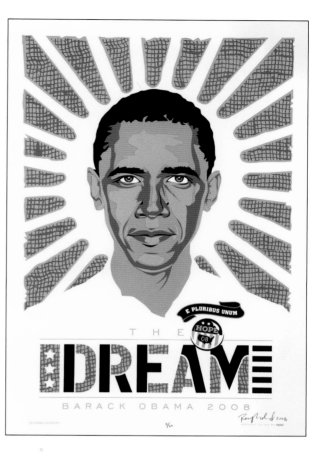

Obama '08 / Vote Change | Thomas Brodahl | 10¼" x 13¼"

Barack Obama | "Zoltron" | 19" x 27"

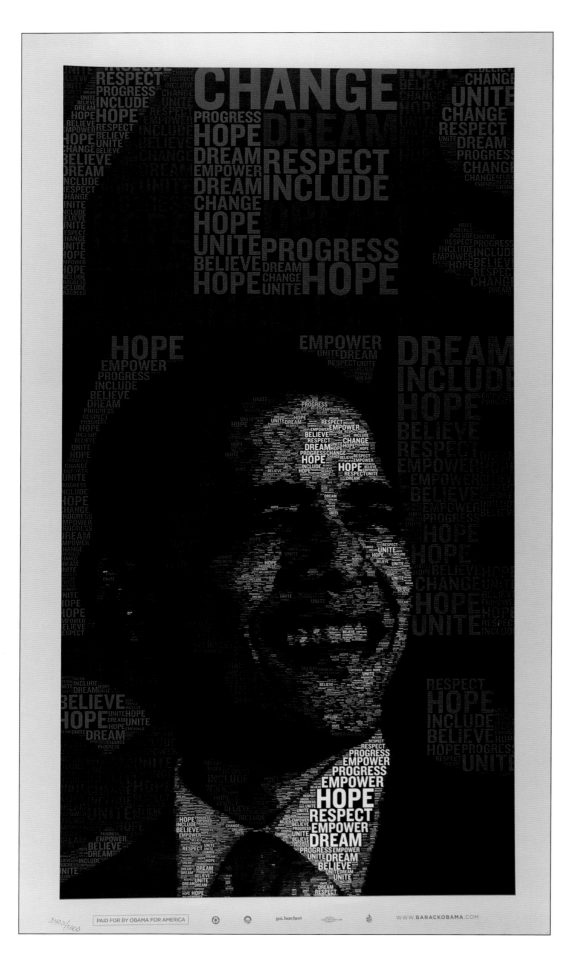

Change | Gui Borchert | 22" x 39½"

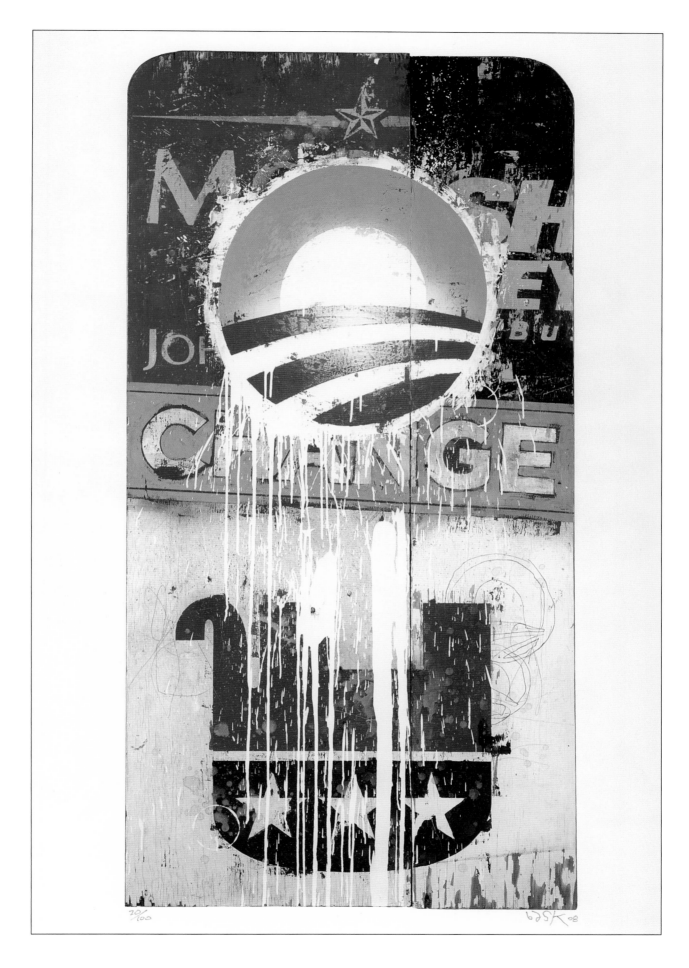

Change We Need | "Bask" | 14½" x 24"

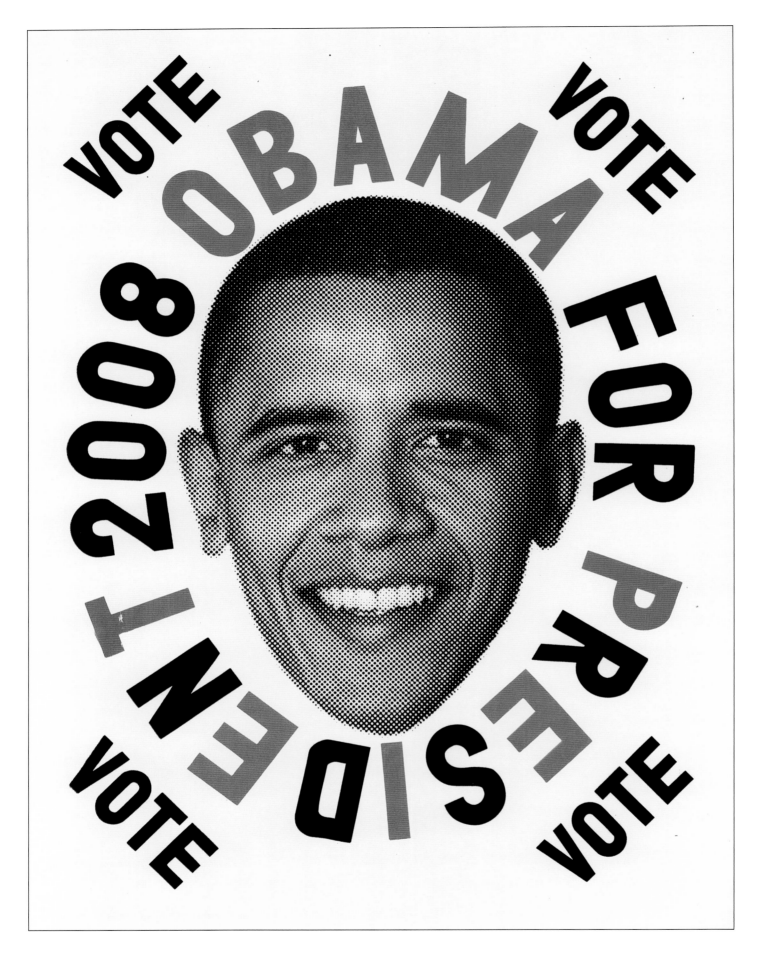

Vote | Print Liberation | 19" x 25"

Obama Extended | Matt Dye | 26" x 40"

Yes We Can | Stephen Fowler | 8" x 16"

Hope | Stephen Fowler | 8" x 16"

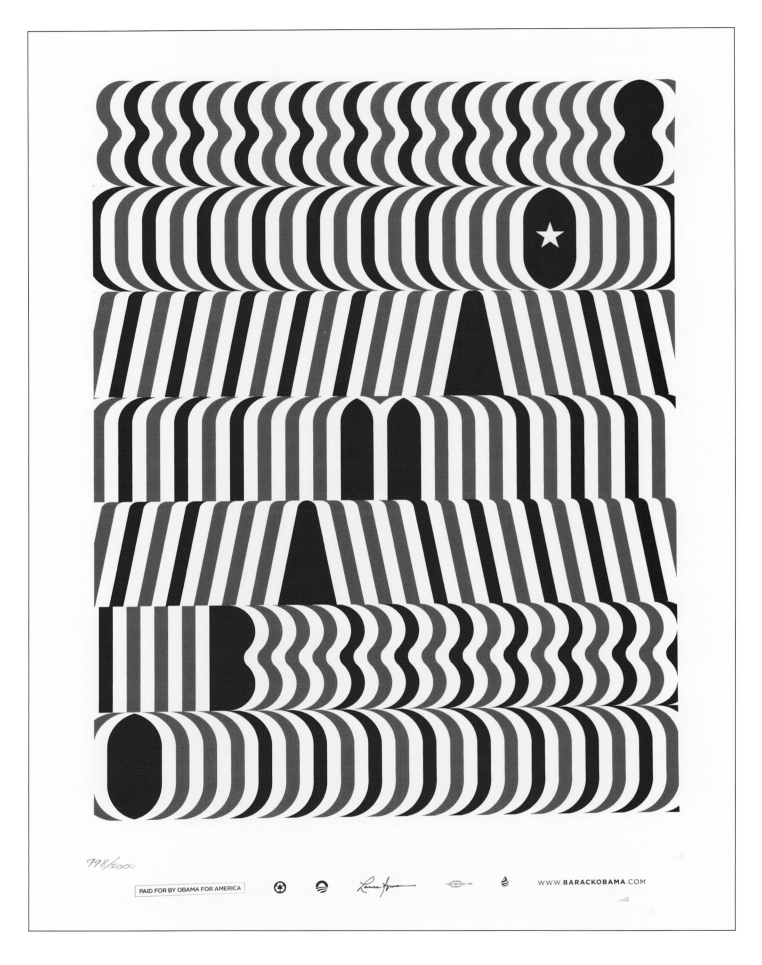

WWW.**BARACKOBAMA**.COM

Obama '08 | Lance Wyman | 25" x 33¼"

Change | Scot Lefavor | 18" x 24"

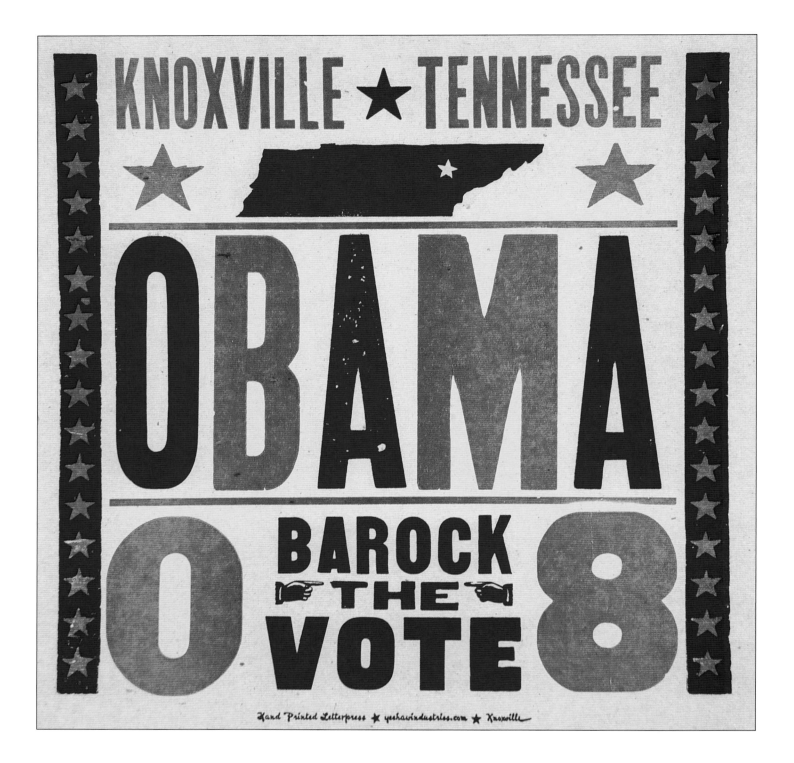

Barock the Vote | Kevin Bradley / Yee-Haw Industries | 16" x 16¼"

Yes We Can | Antar Dayal | 25" x 39½"

Change We Can Believe In | Christopher Cox | 24" x 36"

70/200

Hope | Robert Indiana | 19" x 25"

Obama 2008 | Vonda Sisneros | 17" x 11"

Change | Anthony Armstrong | 24" x 18"

Clean | Jon-Paul Bail | 23" x 35"

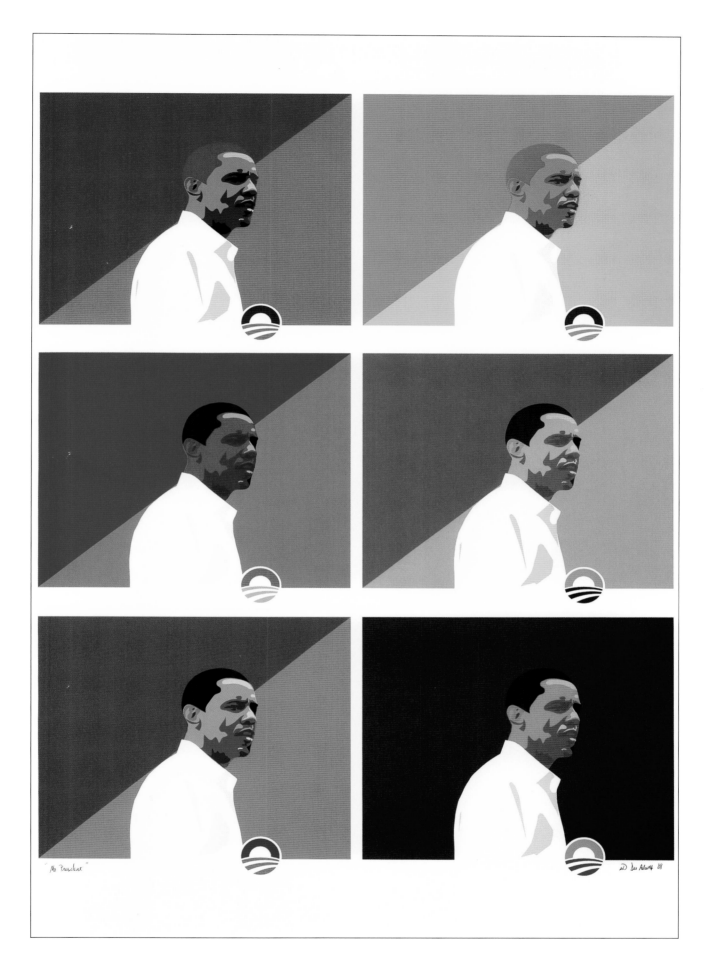

Mr. President | "deedee9:14" | 24¼" x 36"

Vote Early, Rock Late | Caleb Halter | 12½" x 19¾"

Yes We Can | Eileen Burke | 12½" x 18"

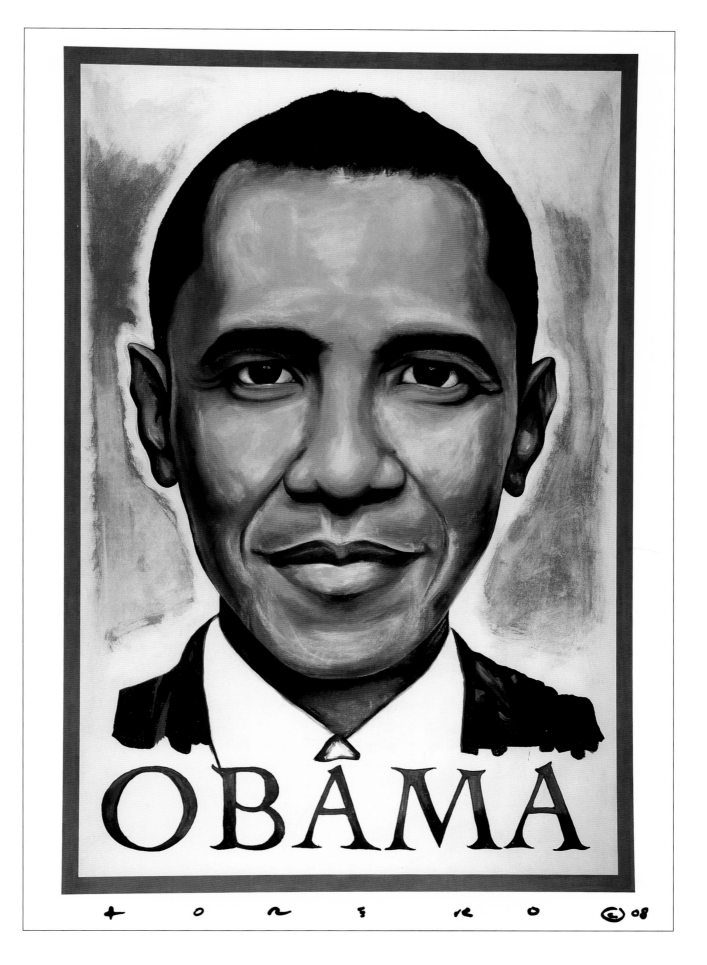

Obama | Mario Torero | 16¼" x 23½"

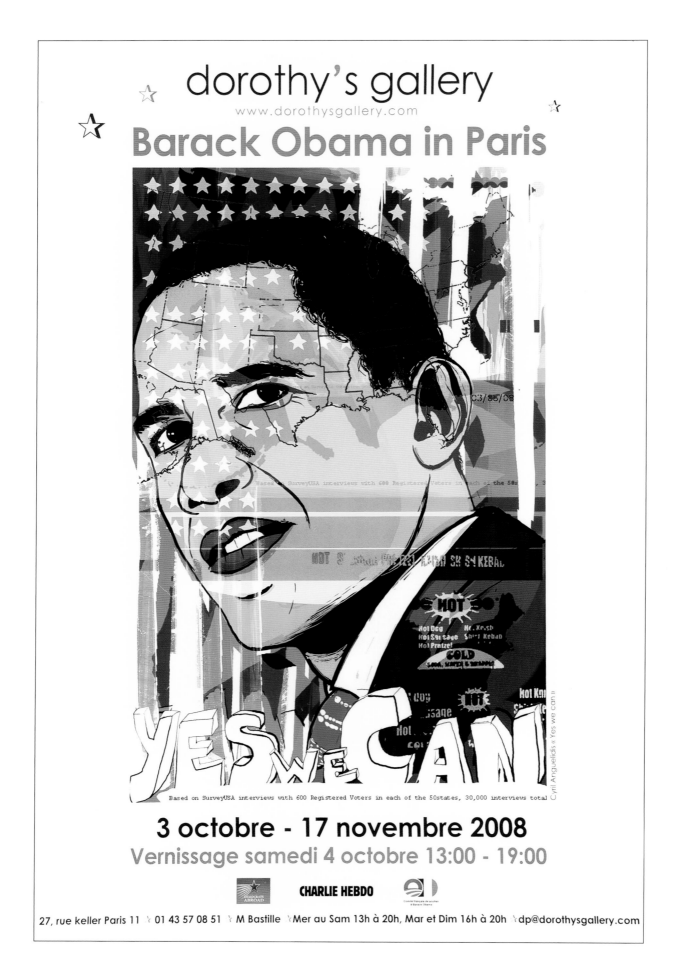

Barack Obama in Paris | Emmanuelle Fevre | 15¾" x 23½"

Si Se Puede | "The Date Farmers" | 18" x 24"

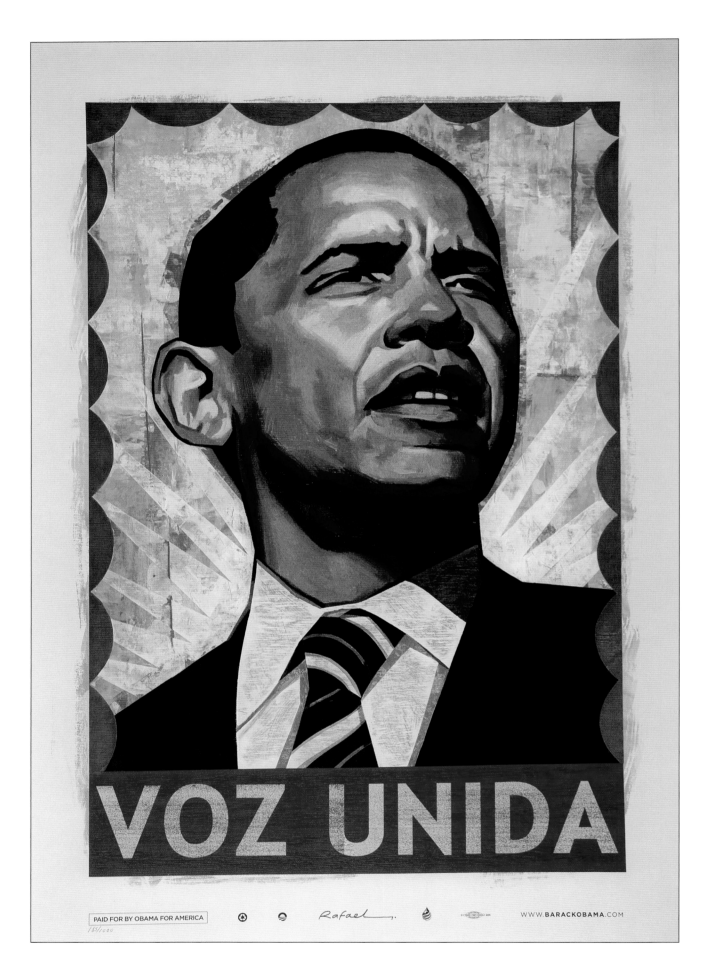

Voz Unida | Rafael Lopez | 25" x 36"

Forward | "Eddie" | 36" x 48"

131/200

One | Justin Bua | 18" x 24"

Change Obama '08 | Benjamin Kuehn | 18" x 24"

Untitled | Billi Kid | 21" x 21"

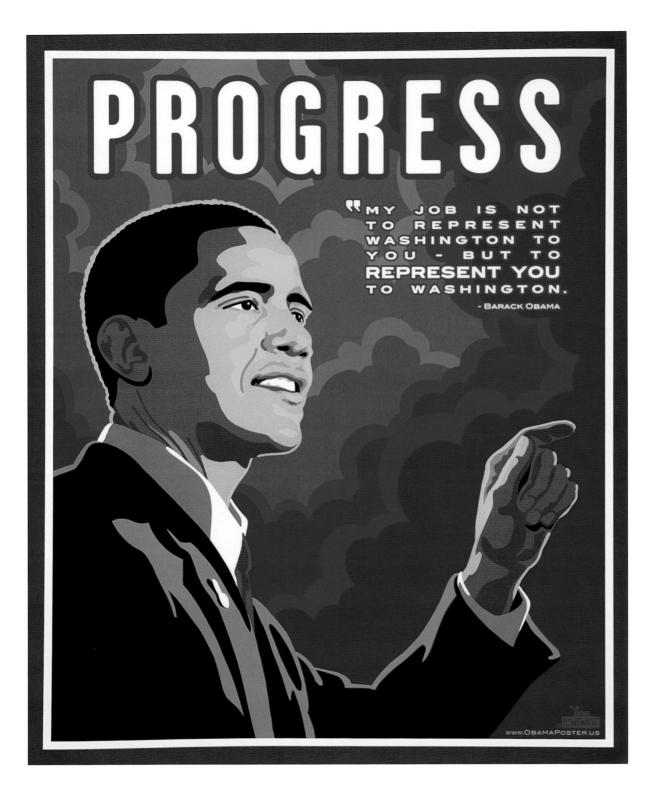

Progress | Steve Lowtwait | 16" x 21½"

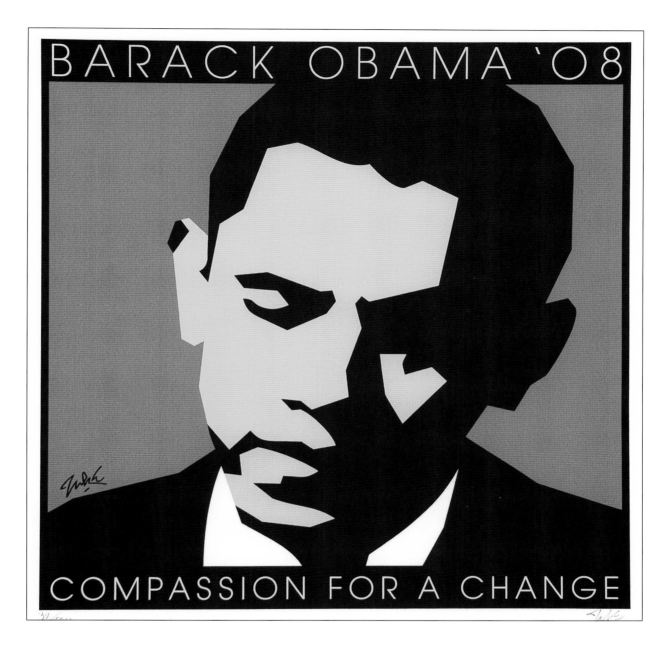

Compassion for a Change | Guy Juke | 13" x 13"

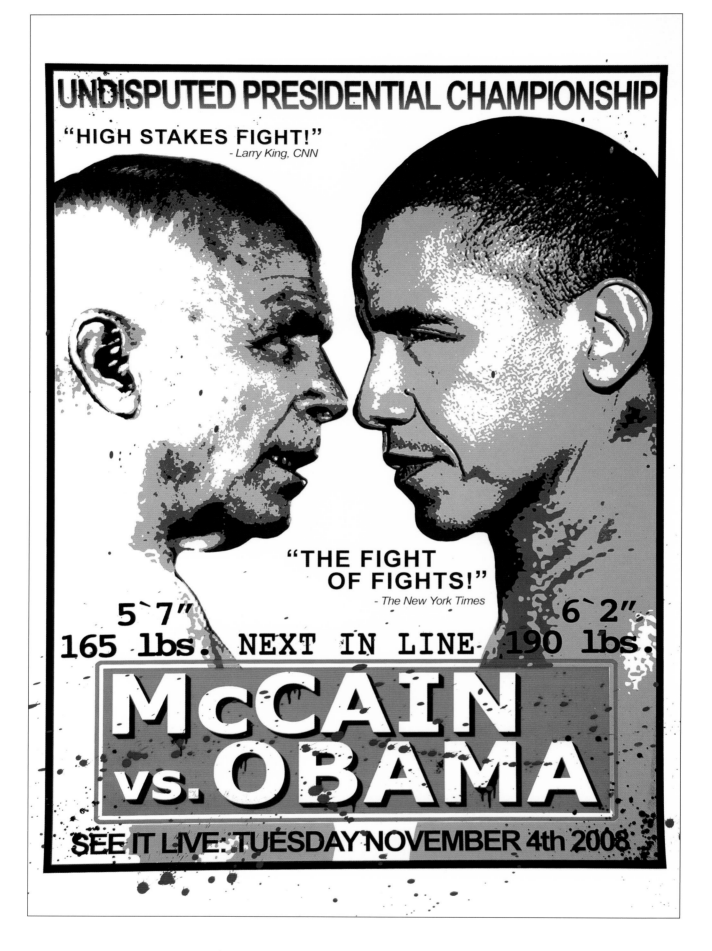

Obama vs. McCain | "Mr. Brainwash" | 25" x 35"

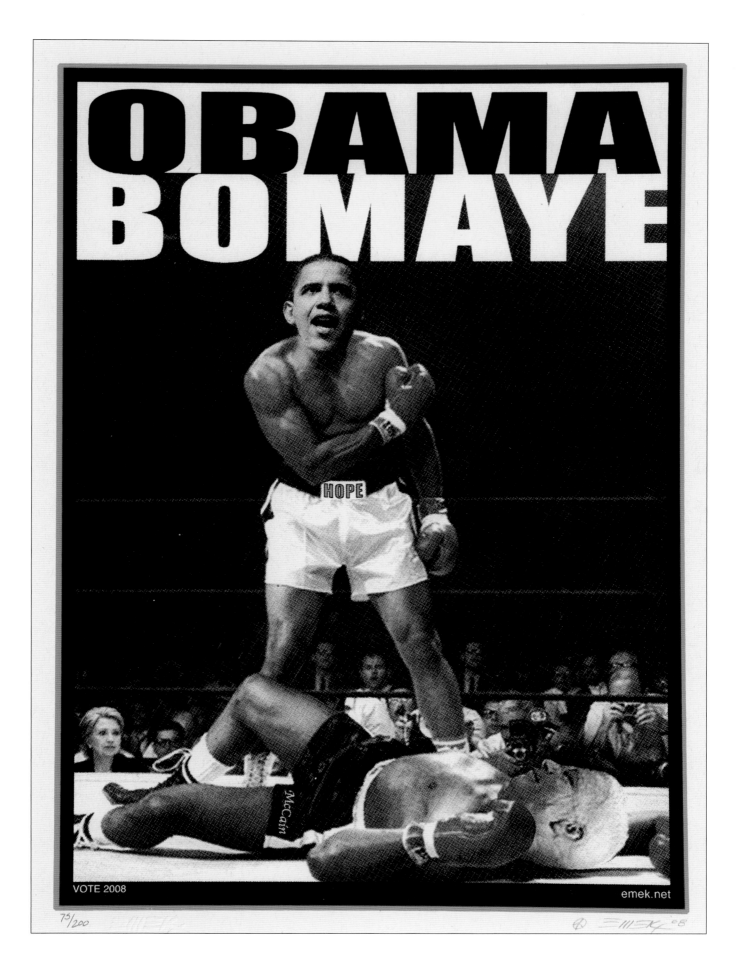

Obama Bomaye | "EMEK" | 11¾" x 16"

Super Obama | Alex Ross | 11" x 14"

Change We Can Believe In | Official Obama Campaign | 11" x 17"

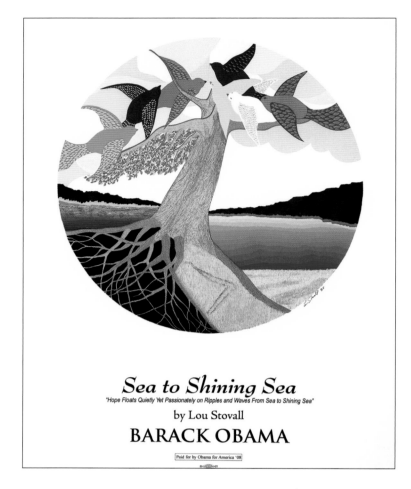

Sea to Shining Sea | Lou Stovall | 16" x 20"

Obama / Biden | Lou Stovall | 11" x 16"

Obama 2008 | Lindsey Kuhn | 18" x 24"

That One | Justin Hampton | 26" x 38¼"

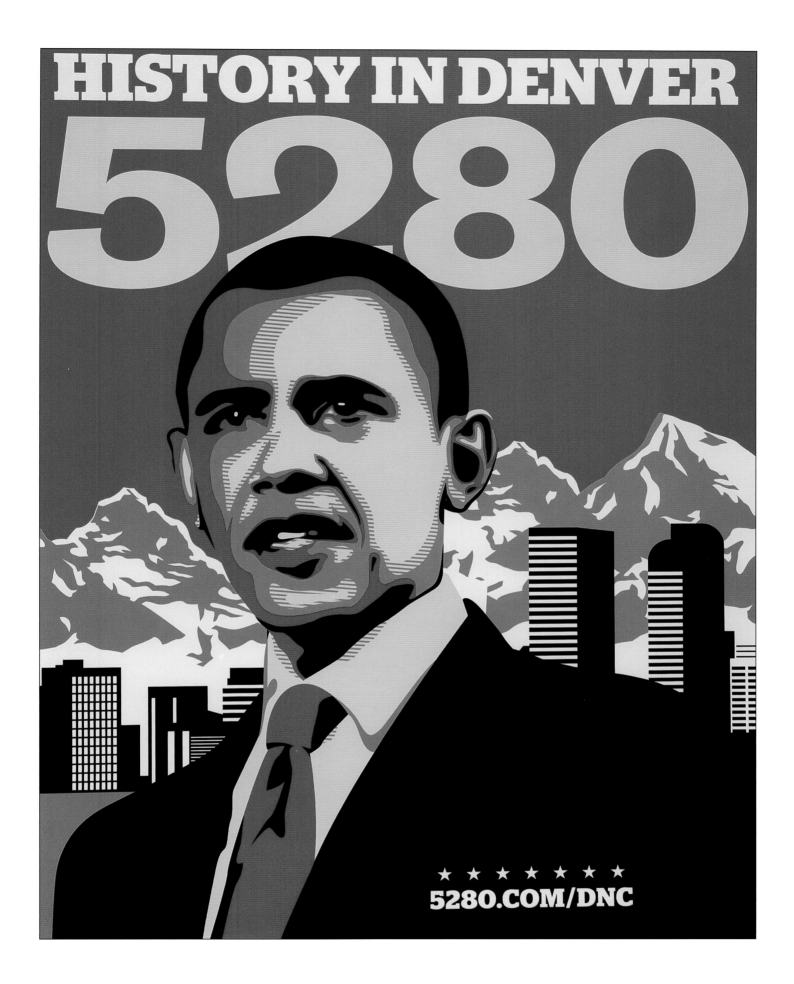

History in Denver 5280 | Shepard Fairey | 22" x 28"

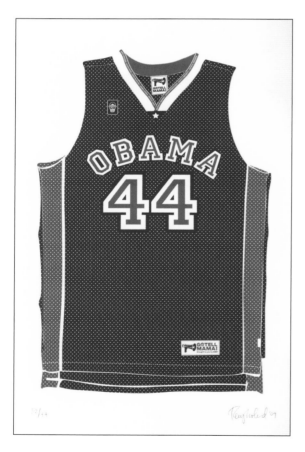

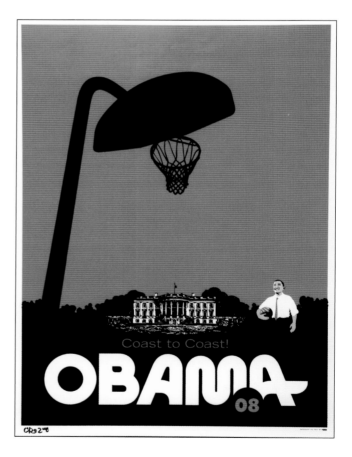

(top left) **Team Obama** | Ray Noland | 18" x 24"
(top right) **Obama Balance** | Ray Noland | 18" x 24"
(bottom left) **Team Obama Jersey 44** | Ray Noland | 24" x 36"
(bottom right) **Coast to Coast** | Ray Noland | 19" x 24"

Change | Derek Hess | 10½" x 28"

Think Peace / Support the Candidate for Change | Debra Campbell | 11" x 17"

Our Movement | Ray Noland | 24" x 36"

"Warrior Politics"

Macaluso 2008

926/3500 David Macaluso 9-27-2008

Warrior Politics | David Macaluso | 16" x 20"

Obama | "Eddie" | 25" x 32"

Untitled | "Snuffhouse" | 18" x 24"

I chose to run for the presidency at this moment in history because I believe deeply that we cannot solve the challenges of our time unless we solve them together — unless we perfect our union by understanding that we may have different stories, but we hold common hopes; that we may not look the same and we may not have come from the same place, but we all want to move in the same direction — towards a better future for our children and our grandchildren.

This belief comes from my unyielding faith in the decency and generosity of the American people. But it also comes from my own American story. It's a story that hasn't made me the most conventional candidate. But it is a story that has seared into my genetic makeup the idea that this nation is more than the sum of its parts — that out of many, we are truly one.

(Excerpts from Barack Obama's speech on race, Philadelphia, March 18, 2008)

Untitled | Tim Hinton | 30" x 20"

Hope / Change | "HVW8" | 19" x 25"

Untitled | Gabe Usadel | 19" x 28"

Untitled | The Half and Half | 19" x 26"

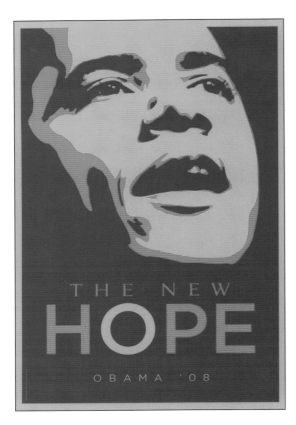

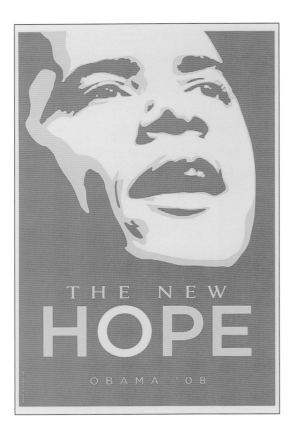

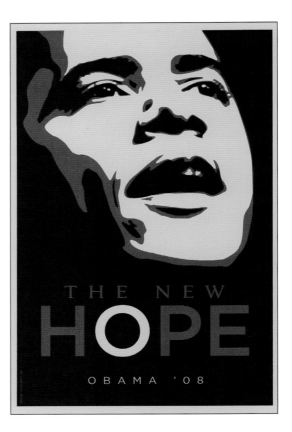

The New Hope | Deroy Peraza | Each 16" x 24"

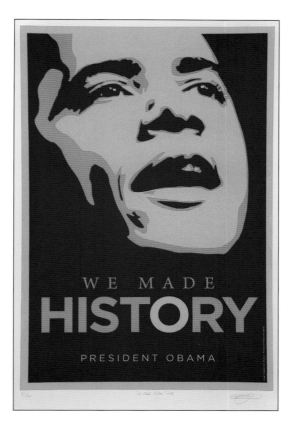
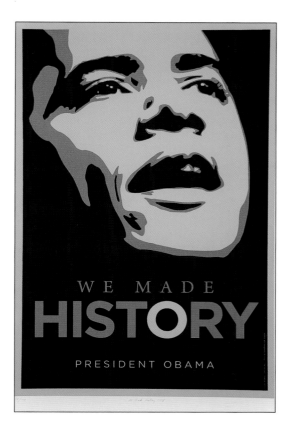
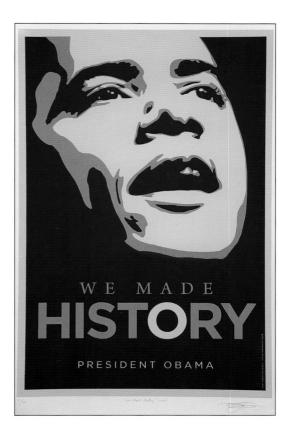
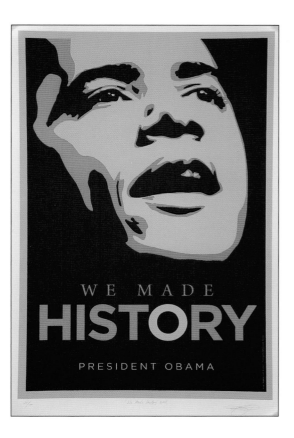

We Made History | Deroy Peraza | Each 16" x 24"

Hope | Alex Pardee | 18" x 24"

Hope | Shepard Fairey | 15" x 22¼"

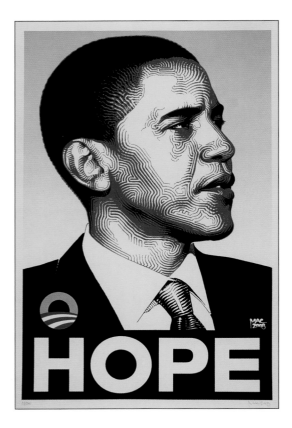

Hope | "The Mac" | 24" x 36"

Hope | David Choe | 18" x 24"

Hope | Amy Martin | 24" x 36"

Victory | Deroy Peraza | 16" x 24"

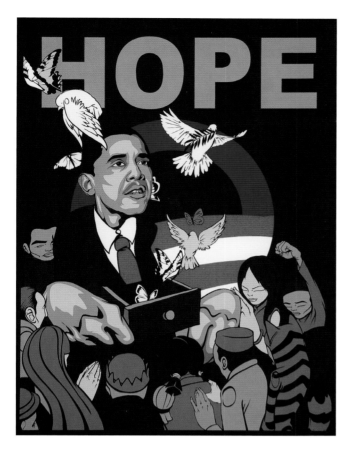

Hope | Sam Flores | 18" x 24"

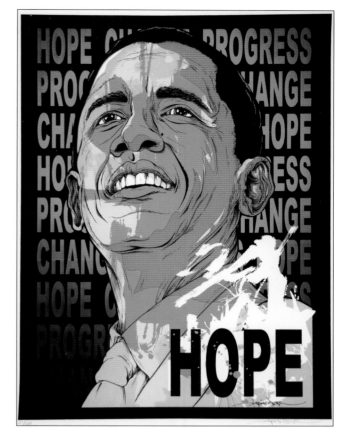

Hope | Alex Pardee | 18" x 24"

Hope | Franke | 24" x 36"

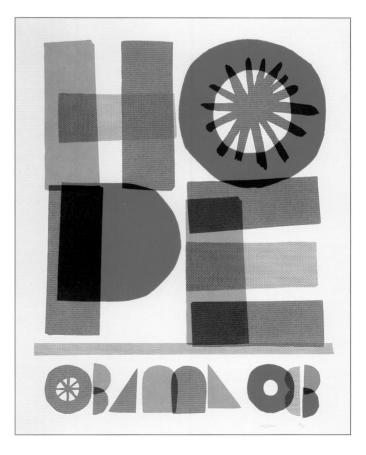

Hope | Cody Hudson | 18" x 24"

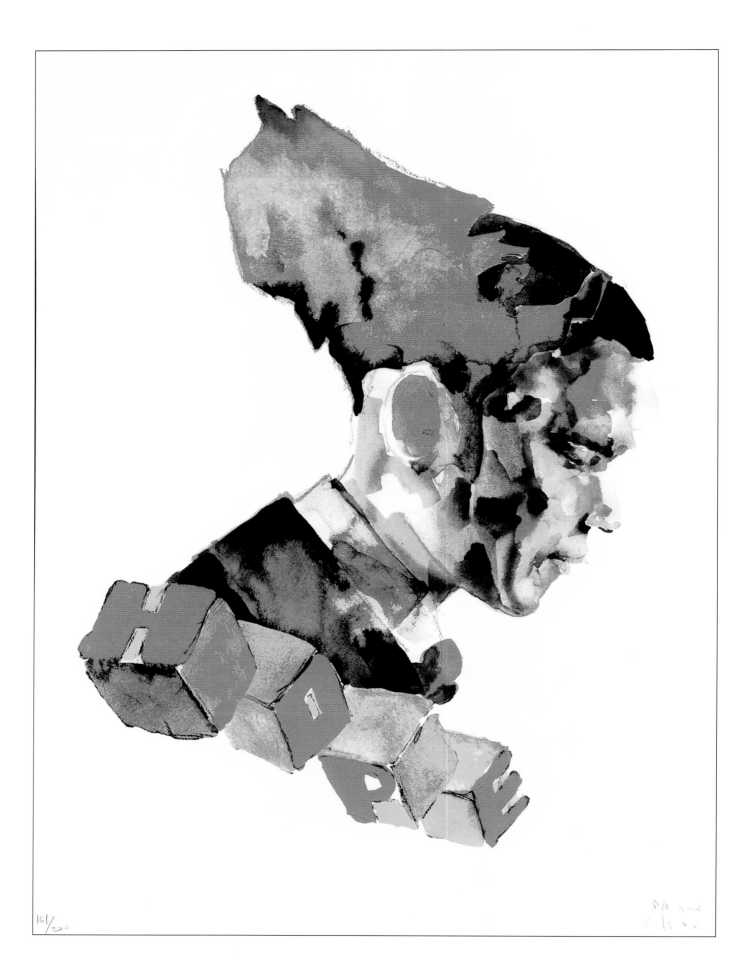

161/200

Hope | David Choe | 18" x 24"

Obama '08 | "Morning Breath" | 18" x 24"

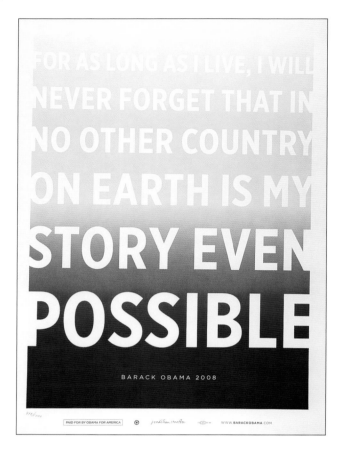

Untitled | Jonathan Hoefler| 25" x 33½"

Obama '08 | Jason H. Phillips | 24" x 36"

Berlin Obama Speech
Official Obama Campaign | 11" x 17"

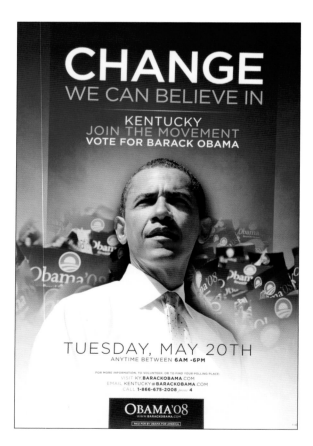

Change | Official Obama Campaign
18" x 24"

PRESIDENT OBAMA

Grant Park - Chicago
November 4, 2008

Grant Park | David Springmeyer | 18" x 24"

Zachary Taylor / Millard Fillmore, 1848
Courtesy Library of Congress

EPILOGUE

THE OUTPOURING OF GUERRILLA STREET art action and eye-catching artistry on display in the posters for the Obama campaign grabbed the attention of the American public. Regardless of political position, Republican, Democrat, Green, Libertarian, or otherwise, people tuned in. The Obama poster phenomenon was truly unprecedented in the annals of U.S. presidential campaigns. However, this was one of a long line of campaigns throughout American history to generate excitement, motivate people to vote, apply the latest technologies, and effectively use posters and other campaign ephemera.

In the 1820s, lithography increasingly made its way to the United States from Germany. Currier and Ives, a company that eventually published 7,500 different titles and over a million prints,

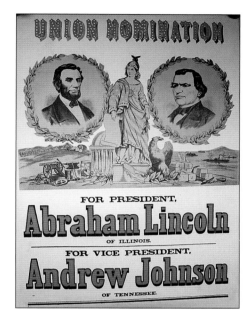

Abraham Lincoln / Andrew Johnson, 1864
Courtesy Hudson Library and Historical Society

began in 1836 to publish hand-colored lithographs of popular pictures, including prints of the major presidential candidates. Take, for example, the company's beautiful 1848 Zachary Taylor and Millard Fillmore print. The campaigns were pleased to be able to market their candidates' images and messages through prints from a growing number of lithographers in a broader and less expensive way. Advances in technology slowly brought the price of lithographic prints in line with letterpress prints, although letterpress color was usually more limited and tended to favor two-color schemes like red and blue. Lithography could also produce beautiful two-color prints, of which the 1864 Abraham Lincoln and Andrew Johnson poster is a prime example.

By the late 1880s hand-coloring processes were largely rendered obsolete by new lithographic techniques. With full-color prints now easier to produce and more widely available, the great age of the modern poster had arrived. Some of the best-designed and most beautiful political posters, as well as the archetypical circus and Wild West show posters of the day, were printed between 1896 and 1912.

In the election battles fought between William McKinley and William Jennings Bryan in 1896 and 1900, colorful poster designs were key weapons. Bryan's electrifying speeches were equally formidable, and McKinley was no match for him in this area. Just as Obama's ability to captivate a crowd has been the envy of his political rivals, such was the case with Bryan's legendary oratory skill.

While historians might argue for years which one of Obama's campaign speeches was his most important, there can be little doubt in Bryan's case. The speech that propelled Bryan on a trajectory that seemed destined for the White House was

Grover Cleveland / Thomas Hendricks, 1884
Courtesy Library of Congress

his Cross of Gold speech at the 1896 Democratic Convention in Chicago, and his posters frequently referenced that pivotal moment. Bryan's speech sent the delegates into a frenzy, and the thirty-six-year-old former congressman from Nebraska won the nomination. He would go on to lose the general election, trying and failing again in 1900 and in 1908, but his rhetorical skills motivated a multitude of faithful supporters who sustained his political ambitions for years after he first appeared on the national stage.

Another new and extremely popular marketing weapon unleashed in this era was the celluloid campaign button invented by Whitehead and Hoag in 1896. Color prints were now reduced to wearable buttons, though some were manufactured as large as twelve inches in diameter and designed to sit atop the parlor side table. The same era also saw the expansion of the silent motion picture industry, and it wasn't long before opportunistic campaigns were distributing film shorts to movie houses of their candidates waddling about, glad-handing the public.

The marketing of Obama as an "everyman" comes from the Age of Jackson in the first part of the nineteenth century. America's egalitarian heritage was well established by the early twentieth century when William Howard Taft was portrayed as just plain friendly "Bill" in a very popular campaign poster. The artist presented Taft as the democratic everyman in a simple and pleasing graphic style.

William Jennings Bryan, 1900
Courtesy Library of Congress

Poster design in America was greatly influenced by European art movements, Art Nouveau, Futurism, de Stijl, Bauhaus, and Russian Constructivism, the latter two favored by the various political ideologies that largely came with European immigrants and later escapees from Nazi

Germany. The development of the offset lithographic process brought cheap graphic materials by the millions to the millions. The American Socialists Party, the Socialists Labor Party, the International Workers of the World (IWW), and magazines like *The New Masses* opposed Woodrow Wilson and the war in cutting-edge graphics. In the 1920s the newly formed Workers Party of America (later Communist Party USA) issued some very powerful, hard-hitting posters aimed at the gut of American capitalism for the William Foster and Benjamin Gitlow campaigns of 1924 and 1928, posters, along with their Soviet counterparts, that have been a source of inspiration to some young street artists for Obama.

The poster continued to enjoy popularity in political campaigns in the 1930s, but technical innovations in communication, including wider use of the telephone and especially the advent of the radio, were making major headway on the campaign trail. President Herbert Hoover understood the political importance of the radio, and was even the first U.S president to appear on television, but it was Franklin Roosevelt who mastered the airwaves with his "fireside chats," during which he projected the warmth of his personality and his charisma into American living rooms. Obama has accomplished much the same thing in his addresses to the nation, where his mastery of the teleprompter gives the impression of a president who will look you in the eye and tell it to you straight.

The New Deal relied heavily on the poster, as did many a government agency in

William McKinley / Theodore Roosevelt, 1900
Courtesy Wisconsin Historical Society

"Bill" (William Howard Taft, 1908)
Author's collection

Vote Communist (CPUSA, 1924)
Hugo Gellert (Courtesy Museum of Democracy)

World War II. Some of the best American poster designers worked in agencies of the Works Progress Administration (WPA) and World War II agencies like the Office of War Information, Treasury Department, and National War Fund. Ben Shahn, a left-wing activist who in the 1930s worked for the WPA, later created a Franklin D. Roosevelt campaign poster for the Democratic National Committee and another issued by Political Action Committee of the Congress for Industrial Organizations. In 1948, Shahn created a famous Progressive Party poster for Henry Wallace's campaign. Entitled *Duo* or *A Good Man is Hard to Find*, the poster depicts Truman and Dewey in a parody of a notorious 1945 *Life* magazine photo of Truman playing a piano adorned by a reclining Lauren Bacall.

After World War II and into the 1950s, the popularity of the poster declined, taking second place to the latest, hottest new media technology—television. The decline, however, was reversed by the blossoming civil rights movement and the escalation of Vietnam War protests. Both movements relied heavily on the poster to further their causes. This baby-boomer revolt, particularly by anti-war activists, expressed itself in the creation of a counterculture—sex, drugs, and rock 'n' roll. The Fillmore and Avalon Ballrooms printed electric-acid, psychedelic gig posters, influenced by Art Nouveau and Jugendstil, in hot colors for hot bands like Country Joe and the Fish, the Jefferson Airplane, and the Steve Miller Blues Band, and by hot artists like Victor

Moscoso and Wes Wilson. Without the Internet and cell phones, the traditional use of handbills and posters served to get the word out quickly.

Eugene McCarthy, a Democratic senator from Minnesota, challenged the current but unpopular President Lyndon Johnson based on a peace platform in the New Hampshire primary in 1968 and did well enough to run Johnson out of the race—the writing was on the wall. Artists and musicians on the left turned out for "Clean Gene," and numbers of innovative posters began to appear. Ben Shahn's classic *McCarthy Peace* is one of the all-time greatest campaign posters. Young Republicans in the Nixon camp also produced a striking poster. The following year, Peter Max stepped in with the first of his many political posters when he created a wordless poster relying entirely on pictures for John Lindsay's 1969 mayoral race.

Senator George McGovern of South Dakota ran as the peace candidate of the Democratic Party in 1972, a year that provides the closest historical precedent for the Obama phenomenon. McGovern, who vigorously opposed the war in Vietnam, surprisingly captured the nomination of a Democratic Party fractured by war, yippies, civil rights

A Good Man
is Hard to Find (1948)
Ben Shahn

McCarthy Peace (Eugene McCarthy, 1968) *Ben Shahn*

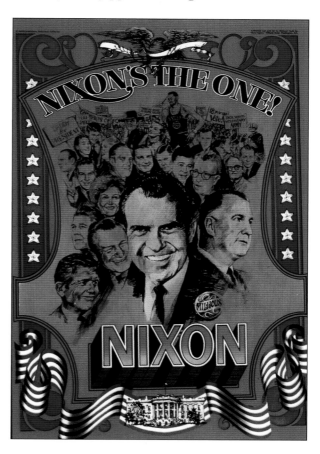

Nixon's the One (Richard M. Nixon, 1968)
J. Michaelson

John Lindsay, 1969
Peter Max

fights, the assassinations of Martin Luther King and Bobby Kennedy, and the disastrous Democratic Convention in Chicago in August 1968. Given these conditions, 1972 was a Republican year, and Richard Nixon appeared unbeatable. Democrats by the tens of thousands defected from the party. But the anti-war movement and those disaffected by the Vietnam quagmire, especially young people and academics, enthusiastically embraced the McGovern candidacy.

Grassroots efforts sprang up across the country, but the McGovern electoral effort was unable to raise sufficient amounts of money, sputtering toward the finish line in November. Nonetheless, enthusiastic artists cranked out hundreds of cheap, well-designed posters, some of which were handmade. Posters of special interest in this graphic mélange include this large, blue-and-white, silkscreen poster with the stenciled shadowing on McGovern's uplifted head, reminiscent of Shepard Fairey's iconic *Hope* poster, though it is doubtful Fairey ever saw it. This attractive and effective poster was hand-printed by the hundreds in the Lincoln, Nebraska, Democratic headquarters. Supporters and volunteers by the dozens waited impatiently for the posters to dry. McGovern headquarters throughout the country were packed with long-haired hippies in tie-dyed T-shirts, bell-bottom pants, and Birkenstocks. More traditional Democrats were there, too. Ironically, these traditionalists tended to be marginalized as posers and wannabes among the new flock of Democrats. The campaign office walls were plastered with multiple layers of political posters, gig posters, and calls for support of multiple causes, especially peace—Haight Ashbury had gone national.

One of the best McGovern gig posters is the Los Angeles concert poster *3/4 for McGovern*, which uses a treble clef and musical notes and features Carole King, Barbara Streisand, and James Taylor. A similarly designed poster features the rock group Chicago, Judy Collins, and Merry Clayton from a San Francisco benefit concert on May 5, 1972, but it was printed in limited numbers and is rarely seen. As with Obama, the rockers and movie stars came out in droves for McGovern, as did a number of famous artists. A Larry Rivers poster, *America Needs McGovern*, was, at the time, on the cutting edge of design and was issued in a signed and numbered, limited edition of one hundred. But of the hundreds of posters for McGovern, the iconic piece was created by Andy Warhol. Underneath a sickly ghoulish green face of Nixon with yellow teeth, the caption reads: "Vote McGovern."

During the early stages of the Obama campaign, when a slew of great posters made their appearance, some political historians warned of a persistent maxim about appealing

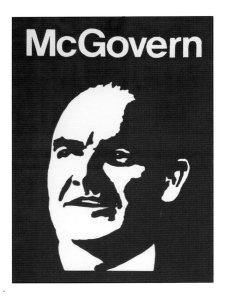

George McGovern, 1972
Author's collection

Together for McGovern (George McGovern, 1972)
Author's collection

Come Home America (George McGovern, 1972)
Author's collection

George McGovern, 1972
Larry Rivers

posters dooming a candidate's chances of election. For instance, McGovern's 1972 posters were once considered the benchmark by which all other campaign posters were judged. In McGovern's case, he carried only Massachusetts and the District of Columbia in losing the Electoral College vote 520 to 17, the worst drubbing in American political history. However, the Obama campaign's exemplary posters would forever put to rest the urban legend equating great poster artwork with political failure.

After the success of the civil rights movement, the end of the war in Vietnam, and the petering out of America's great boomer revolt, the campaign poster once again went into a decline.

The posters that came out of the Gary Hart campaign for the Democratic nomination in 1984 were an exception. Two of note are a poster by Tom W. Benton, who also created the *Hunter Thompson for Sheriff* (of Pitkin County, Colorado) poster, and another by famous pop artist Ed Ruscha. These posters, however, were more a design carryover from the involvement of Hart and Benton in the McGovern campaign than evidence of a rebirth of campaign poster artistry. However, other aspects of culture foreshadowed a comeback for the great campaign poster.

Politics aside, rock 'n' roll in the mid-1980s was undergoing a move to regional diversity. Hundreds of unknown independent bands were in need of promotion, and the death of LPs, whose cover designs often had more artistic merit than the music,

Concert poster (George McGovern, 1972)
Author's collection

left many young and talented graphic artists in need of work.

The screen prints medium for small-batch runs of quality posters was back in fashion, as was the letterpress process, which started taking the art in fresh and creative new directions. No better example of this exists than the work of the Hatch Print Shop (now Hatch Show Print) in Nashville, Tennessee, under the direction of Jim Sherraden. Not all of the new poster makers entering the art world in the 1990s were exclusive gig poster makers; many did fine screen prints for causes and posters with a political bent. Shepard Fairey conducted his now-famous *Andre the Giant* sticker campaign that garnered worldwide attention. Street artists

Vote McGovern (George McGovern, 1972)
Andy Warhol

emerged and began guerrilla nighttime agitprop actions. Graffiti was everywhere in the urban core, and elaborate spray-painted murals were starting to cover the sides of buildings. But, as in the past, the poster revival and street art phenomenon were also tied to a new technology; in this case, the modern computer age and its emphasis on digitalization. The mix proved explosive in terms of its influence on the art world.

Political campaigns again had new methods for producing campaign materials, while popular musicians were increasingly vocal in their support of the candidates.

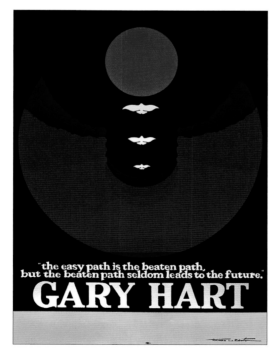

The Easy Path is the Beaten Path
(Gary Hart, 1984)
Tom W. Benton

America Needs Hart
(Gary Hart, 1984)
Author's collection

Bill Clinton, 1992
Author's collection

Win In '96 (Bill Clinton / Al Gore, 1996)
Peter Max

Bill Clinton's 1992 campaign exemplified the new trend of pushing the candidate as a "cool celeb," engendering excitement with the MTV generation. A poster given out to delegates by the Democratic National Committee when they arrived in New York is a perfect example. His 1996 campaign also included many fine examples, none finer than one by Peter Max. As he had done before with the Lindsay poster in 1969, Max did not use the names of the candidates, but included only a simple caption under brown-tone portraits that read *Win in '96!*

Al Gore's run for the presidency in 2000, the closest race in U.S. political history, also generated some exciting posters. A fundraiser in Woodside, California, on April 6, 1999, for Gore featured the Flying Other Brothers (FOB) band and was promoted with a gig-style poster flashing the FOB winged logo. John Kerry and Emek Golan seem an unlikely pairing, but in 2004, the king of rock posters produced a colorful gig poster for a Kerry fundraising concer. Several other benefit concert posters were also worthy of notice; things were picking up, fueled mostly on the left by hatred of George W. Bush.

From the left's perspective, "Dubya" had stolen the 2000 election. When he won again in 2004, few would credit what many experts on both sides acknowledge was a well-organized, well-financed, and brilliantly run campaign. To those who hated him, the inarticulate man who had taken the country to war under false pretenses was worthy only of ridicule and contempt as a failed president. The nation was severely polarized.

Into this volatile mix stepped Illinois Senator Barack Obama, whose 2004 speech turned heads and revived hopes that he was a candidate who could win and take the country in a new direction. Many on the left wing of the party embraced Obama immediately, but the majority of the party looked upon Hillary Clinton as the heir apparent. Powerful women in the Democratic Party were committed to having her be the first female nominee of a major party, and chances were very good she would be president.

Obama's credentials with the left on the major issues were already impeccable by the time he announced his candidacy on the steps of the Lincoln Memorial in Springfield, Illinois. He had opposed the war in Iraq from the start, he opposed the surge, and he promised to extract the country from another quagmire. Better yet, he was an articulate mixed-race American who understood the younger generation. The candidate inspired the young and reignited the passions of aging boomers as had John F. Kennedy, Martin Luther King, Bobby Kennedy, Eugene McCarthy, and George McGovern. Hillary Clinton was never a contender among this idealistic group of voters, and her supporters included few from the outsider art crowd. Of three noteworthy Hillary posters, two were created by Tony Puryear, the well-known Hollywood script writer and illustrator, and the other by Omaha gig poster maker Fred Hosman for the

Fundraiser concert for Al Gore, 2000
Author's collection

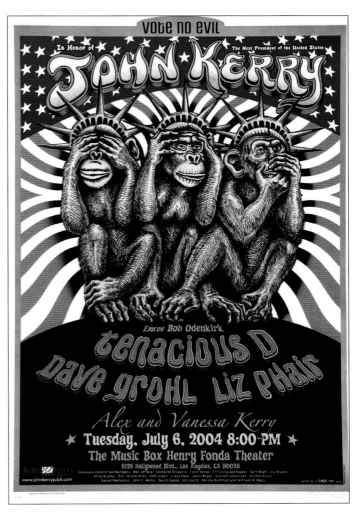

John Kerry, 2004
Emek Golen

Hillary Clinton, 2008
Tony Puryear

Nebraska primary. Other than these three examples, artistic excellence in posters and prints tilted heavily in Obama's favor.

As we now know, Obama would go on to win the nomination with the overwhelming support of the left and the young. Among the young were a group of outsider, hip-hop, skateboarder, guerrilla artists who committed early to their candidate, bringing with them both their talent and a host of newfangled communication devices. Some art critics suggest that this marks the beginning of a new paradigm, that the Obama art phenomenon will lead to a rejuvenated American art movement. In the unprecedented poster action for Obama we see a combination of the poster revival that began in the 1980s, the latest in digital technology, and one candidate's ability to convincingly sell a dream of progress, change, and of course, hope.

Clinton / Obama, 2044
Shannon Moore

ACKNOWLEDGMENTS

First and foremost, I wish to thank all of the artists who granted their permission to include the posters and prints in this book, and I'm grateful to the many who also generously shared their high-resolution files. Ron and Terssa English were particularly helpful in this regard, and I am appreciative of their support. This book would not have been possible had it not been for the many services rendered by my assistant, Robert Heishman. Robert undertook the digital photography for nearly all of the posters in the book. Thank you, Robert. A special thanks also goes to Ray Noland, who kindly wrote the foreword to this volume and invited me to help arrange and locate the posters for Officially Unofficial: Inspired Posters for Obama, Chicago Exhibition 2009, which ran at the Chicago Tourism Center April 1–May 31, 2009. Nathan Mason, Chicago Department of Cultural Affairs, made it possible for me to bring a van-load of posters to the Windy City. Ken Harman of the Obama Art Report also helped arrange the Chicago show, and he did yeoman service in helping to track down artists and their posters. To all those at the Kansas City Art Institute who assisted in various ways, thank you. President Kathleen Collins, the board, and Vice-President for Academic Affairs Mark Salmon made possible a sabbatical and several faculty development grants. Phyllis Moore, my department chair, supported my publishing venture into posters from the start, as did Carl Kurtz, professor in School of the Foundation Year. Tilly Woodward, outreach curator for the Faulconer Gallery at Grinnell College also encouraged me to proceed. For encouragement and proofreading I am indebted for a second time to Robert W. and Mary Anne Demeritt. Marc Deckard, photo/digital film technician, kindly agreed to print out some of the high-resolution files as a test of quality. Rachell Smith and her staff of Beverly Adhern, Michael Schonhoff, and Owen Martin recognized the importance and the novelty of the Obama posters early on and helped arrange a first showing at the Upper Gallery, H&R Block Art Space. Owen Martin curated this well-attended show, which ended up running for nearly five months. Tracy Abein, editor, and Sonya Baughman, art director, of *Review Magazine* were kind enough to publish my essay "Barackstreet Art: Outsider, Hip Hop and Guerrilla, Unprecedented Poster Action for Obama" in the September 2008 issue. The same article with different poster illustrations is online at www.review-magazine.org. Alex Stock, former student, friend, and Osage Indian princess, at the very last minute helped find Ryan Red Corn and secure his permission. I also wish to thank the management team at Zenith Press who saw early on the artistic merit of this Obama material and were genuinely excited about publication. Few publishers would have taken this risk. Steve Gansen, my editor at Zenith Press, worked with me on a daily basis to meet a series of unmerciful deadlines. With only a few false starts, we accomplished our goal. Thank you, Steve. Finally, a deep debt of gratitude is owed to my agent, Fritz Heinzen, who always surprises me with how quickly he places my books.

Not all artists who made an Obama poster or print were included in this volume. The selection was difficult, and there are, I assume, dozens of posters that I simply didn't know existed. Others were not included because their creators failed to answer my e-mail requests to participate or their offers arrived too late. Let me know about your posters and prints, and there is a good chance they may make a future edition. Contact me at hwert@sbcglobal.net. Thank you. Lastly, any mistakes that occur are solely my responsibility.

CATALOG OF POSTERS AND PRINTS

Nicholas Rock

Page 6: Nicholas Rock, who lives and works in Providence, Rhode Island, was attracted to the unity message in so many of Obama's speeches, and his *Unite Us 2008* poster was the result. Entered into the art contest held by the Manifest Hope Gallery in Denver, Rock was one of the five winners. After Denver, the print traveled to Italy to be part of Roma per Obama, a display of Obama art sponsored by the Democratic Party of Italy. Printed by wind power on recycled paper by well-known printmaker Jay Zehngebot as a signed-and-numbered limited edition of fifty, *Unite Us 2008* quickly sold out.

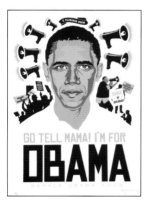

Ray Noland

Page 8: Ray Noland used his anonymity and guerrilla street artist's tactics to build interest in the Obama campaign to create a buzz around his home base of Chicago. This thirty-something artist is a graduate of the School of the Art Institute of Chicago, a printmaker, and an early and enthusiastic supporter of Obama. This print of his exuberant *Go Tell Mama!* design was released in a second signed-and-numbered limited edition run of ninety.

Eddie

Page 17: Disillusioned with politics as usual, the artist who simply goes by the name Eddie was attracted to Obama's character. One night on his computer he turned out a poster design rather like Shepard Fairey's. There it sat for three months until one day he showed the design to his friend Moy, who responded, "You gotta make these." He did, and the two soon started pasting them up throughout the Bay area. Posters appeared on freeway off-ramps, BART tunnel entrances, utility boxes, newspaper boxes, and the Bay Bridge. In Eddie's later Obama posters, he took his method a step further to complete reliance on pictorial imagery—no words. This poster incorporates the color brown effectively and conveys that Obama speaks for the country and for its future.

Jessica Hische

Page 18: Jessica Hische is a well-known Brooklyn illustrator who received a BFA from the Tyler School of Art, Temple University. She claims to be influenced by "popsicle-stick jokes, terribly wonderful action movies, hearty meals, trashy celebrity news, my friends, Victorian and other vintage type paper, and books on tape." Wedded to her computer, candy bars, and coffee, she turns out bold, colorful imagery that has the feel of being hand drawn. Her *Brooklyn for Barack* gig poster is an open, offset edition.

Kathleen Judge

Page 19: Poster artist Kathleen Judge created this signed-and-numbered limited-edition screen print of 236 along with Steve Walters, sometimes known as the godfather of gig posters, for an Obama fundraiser at the famous Chicago club the Hideout. The posters were given out that evening to the contributors as they mingled and listened to the music of Andrew Bird and Dianogah.

Tom Slaughter

Page 20: Born in 1955 in New York City, Tom Slaughter received his B.A. from Connecticut College and quickly went on to establish himself as a premier artist, designer, and printmaker. He began by exhibiting his work in 1983 with a show at the Drawing Center of New York. Since then he has had twenty solo exhibitions in countries around the world—Cologne, Germany; London, England; Fukuoka, Japan; and Vancouver, Canada—and his work has been purchased by the Museum of Modern Art in New York and the Whitney Museum. This red-and-white print and its blue-and-white counterpart were each released in signed-and-numbered screen-print editions of fifty.

Eddie

Page 21: *New Era* portrays the radical change that the younger generation expects from its president in a hip, humorous, and effective way.

Nick Toga

Page 22: A Californian since birth and now a resident of Los Angeles, Nick Toga fell in love with design in high school when he began experimenting with Photoshop. Committed to graphic design, he attended the Art College Center of Design in Pasadena. Presently he is a designer at Fresh Pressed, a public screen-printing shop in Los Feliz, California. His screen print, *East LA Portrait*, in a signed edition that was printed in both a dark-blue and a light-blue version. Toga cleverly uses a map of the United States to demonstrate that Obama stands for and unites all of America.

Lashun Tines

Page 23: Lashun Tines says that his mother taught him to trace Marvel comic book superheroes at an early age. This led him to begin experimenting with drawing and writing his own comics and creating his own characters. In college he majored in creative writing, photography, illustration, and journalism. Forced to decide, he finally chose graphic design, since he thought this was how he could best incorporate all of his interests in one field. He presently designs for Creative Circle. *Get It Straight, Obama in '08* is an open-edition giclée print.

Official Obama Campaign

Page 24: *I Want You to Caucus* trades on one of the most famous poster images of all time: James Montgomery Flagg's classic World War I poster of Uncle Sam pointing and proclaiming "I Want You." Striking and effective poster design never dies when the images are repeatedly appropriated. Flagg himself did spin-offs for Franklin Roosevelt and for various World War II organizations. However, some important differences need to be noted with the Obama version. The poster is not in a patriotic red, white, and blue; Obama is not dressed in an Uncle Sam suit; and his dress is casual, no tie and an open coat. Still, almost all who view poster recognize its historical roots in one form or another.

Julian Norman

Page 25: *Obama Is Money* has proven a popular poster in a signed-and-numbered limited edition of one thousand. Given the amount of money that the Obama campaign raised, this poster has an unintended double meaning.

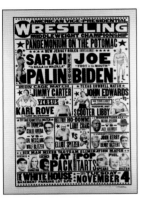

Kevin Bradley

Page 26: Kevin Bradley, Yee-Haw Industries, demonstrating his wonderful sense of humor and his artistic talent, created *American Presidential Wrestling Heavyweight Championship* and, shown here, *American Vice-Presidential Wrestling Middleweight Championship*. A retro takeoff on letterpress wrestling posters of the 1950s and '60s, Bradley has headliner presidential contenders and politicians battling for high-stakes prizes in these star-studded main events. The middleweight championship poster, featuring Palin versus Biden, was released on the Yee-Haw website in a signed-and-numbered limited edition of 150.

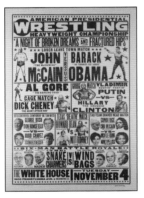

Kevin Bradley

Page 27: *American Presidential Wrestling Heavyweight Championship* features McCain versus Obama, as well as matches between a host of wannabes and has-beens—this is print political satire at its best in the tradition of *The Onion*. Like its companion piece, the heavyweight championship poster was released in a signed-and-numbered limited edition of 150.

Wes Winship

Page 28: Wes Winship and Mike Davis are the co-owners and creative drive behind Burlesque of North America, a premier print studio that has turned out nothing but high-quality work, many hotly collected gig posters. First successes included screen prints for a band named Fog as well as for Minneapolis clubs First Avenue and Triple Rock Social Club. Burlesque also published all the screen prints for the Upper Playground series and printed three gorgeous, signed, limited-edition prints of Ron English's *Abraham Obama*: a gold print in a run of fifteen, and maroon and copper prints in editions of six each. Winship's colorful contribution as an artist to the Upper Playground series was printed in a signed-and-numbered limited edition of two hundred. Burlesque is a collective of artists that divides its time between creating rock concert posters as a group and supporting the work of individual artists within the group.

Guy Juke

Page 29: Artist Guy Juke, a.k.a. Blackie White, arrived in Austin, Texas, in 1973. The following year the famous poster/print shop Armadillo recognized his talents and asked him to come aboard. Juke did, and shortly he was creating some of the most colorful, imaginative, and eclectic screen-print posters in a town about to explode onto the art and music scene. *President Barack Obama, Stand with Me* marks Obama's election victory, and this print is a signed-and-numbered limited-edition screen print.

Sol Sender

Page 30: Sol Sender, Andy Keene, and Amanda Gentry, a Chicago design team, created a wildly successful Obama campaign logo that graphically encapsulated the ideas associated with hope and change. The resulting blue half circle over the three curved red stripes clearly suggests the sun rising over the earth, the dawn of a new day. A signed-and-numbered limited-edition screen print of 365 was offered by the Danziger Projects gallery in New York. It should be remembered that "W" was a winning iconic logo for the savvy Bush team in 2004. The rule—keep it simple, dummy.

Antar Dayal

Page 31: *Change We Can Believe In* at first looked to rival Shepard Fairey's images, but, while popular, it never gained the traction it deserved. Antar Dayal released the print in signed-and-numbered giclée editions on his website in three sizes, the smaller versions in print runs of 480 and the huge, 43x57-inch version in a run of 60. The AFSCME Regional Council in Ohio distributed an offset edition with the AFSCME logo attached. Dayal, in the midst of a late-summer poster flurry, suffered a tragedy when the raging hill fires around Santa Barbara destroyed 250 homes, including his house and studio. Demonstrating an irrepressible spirit, Dayal almost immediately began to create beautiful new prints. Shepard Fairey, the Obama Art Report, and a bevy of artists came to his rescue.

David Macaluso

Page 33: David Macaluso dropped out of Parsons The New School for Design in 1994 to pursue other interests. He says that for years he did not even pick up a pencil to draw. Occasionally people knew of his abilities, and he would take a commission or draw something for a friend, but he hung back from a commitment to art-making, unconvinced of its worthiness. After all, what was there to express? Born to an artistic family that came from northern Italy in 2005, Macaluso eventually gave into his talent and returned to painting. In *Color in the Mind's Eye*—a signed-and-numbered limited-edition giclée print of 1,500—Macaluso captures a forward-looking, contemplative Obama in an oil rendering.

Official Obama Campaign

Page 34: This particular poster, featuring Michelle Obama and entitled *Vote for Change*, was distributed in another must-win state—Ohio. A photo of a warm, open, convivial Michelle, a woman who can stand alone, countered early criticism of the candidate's wife and successfully reassured voters.

T. R. Red Corn

Page 35: T. R. Red Corn grew up on the Osage Nation Reservation in Pawhuska, Oklahoma, and in Lenexa, Kansas. At the University of Kansas he received a BFA degree in visual communications with an emphasis in graphic design. His prodigious amount of work has been influenced by artists like Woody Crumbo, Loren Pahsetopah, Jayson BraveHeart, Oscar Howe, Jerome Tiger, Raymond Red Corn Jr., and Jim Red Corn. Red Corn is also an admirer of a long list of contemporary artists that includes Rose Bean Simpson, Monty Singer, Ryan Singer, Micah Wesley, Jeremy Fields, America Meredith, Chris Pappan, Bunky EchoHawk, and Banksy. *Democratic Convention 2008, Native Nations United for Change* was created to publicize the Native American Platform Summit at the Democratic National Convention and was released in a signed-and-numbered limited edition. After the election, an orange version of the poster was selected by the Smithsonian for its Inaugural Festival.

Java John Goldacker

Page 36: A Florida artist who has a local National Public Radio show on WFIT called *An Acoustic Record*, "Java John" Goldacker's poster catches the retro heart of the traditional Cypress Garden's School of Florida advertising. Goldacker was born in New Jersey but grew up in southern Florida, where he spent much of his time drawing. More recently he illustrated the children's book *River Dragon*. His work has been published in *Photoshop Creative* magazine and *PHANART: The Art of the Fans of Phish*. A unique feature of this signed, open-edition poster is that it is autographed by candidate Obama on the palm tree in the upper right-hand corner.

Unknown artist

Page 37: This St. Louis, Missouri, poster, an open-edition giclée, has it all. Flag bunting, Harry Truman, the Eero Saarinen arch, the old courthouse, the city portrayed as a frontier town—St. Louis is the gateway to the West.

Ray Noland

Page 38: Ray Noland created this poster for the Chicago Obama show Officially Unofficial: The Inspired Art for Obama that ran from April 1 to May 31 at the Chicago Tourism Center. The show, well received, was put together by Noland; Scott Thomas, former design director of Obama for America; Nathan Mason, Chicago Department of Cultural Affairs; Ken Harman, Obama Art Report; and Hal Elliott Wert, Kansas City Art Institute. Noland created two screen prints—one available as a limited, signed number of artist's proofs, 18 x 24 inches, and the other a larger 22½ x 29-inch version in a signed-and-numbered limited edition of forty-four.

Benjamin Kuehn

Page 39: Benjamin Kuehn was on board early with his Obama poster designs that could be purchased from his website store or on eBay. A portrait *Hope* poster was followed by *Words We Can Believe In*, printed in two sizes of signed-and-numbered limited editions of fifty. Kuehn is an up-and-coming marketing and design professional from Minneapolis. He was among the first artists to support Obama, and he has sold out fifteen separate print runs.

Ray Noland

Page 40: This poster advertises Ray Noland's Go Tell Mama! show in Raleigh, North Carolina. These special events were not your usual campaign rallies. Held in art galleries that featured Noland's and local artists' Obama artwork, these events always had music, sometimes featured performances, and were occasionally followed by forays into the night to plaster up posters in documented and interesting ways. Noland put together shows in Texas, Pennsylvania, North Carolina, California, and Georgia. Show posters were sometimes printed on a heavy cardboard or were screen prints on cheap paper.

Eddie

Page 41: A blow-up of the upper area of the Eddie poster series, this poster was almost always printed out large.

Ron English

Pages 42–44: San Francisco publishing house Last Gasp pitches Ron English, author of *Popaganda*, as "one of the seminal figures in the ever-growing culture jamming movement." He has pirated over one thousand billboards over the last twenty years, replacing existing advertisements with his own "subvertisements" that demonstrate the emptiness of modern bourgeois culture. English has circumnavigated the globe committing "art crimes." His spectrum-colored portraits of "Abraham Obama," a fusion between portraits of Abraham Lincoln and Barack Obama, printed on vinyl, gained nationwide acclaim when they appeared in Boston, in Los Angeles, and at the Democratic National Convention in Denver. His first *Abraham Obama* in black-and-white, a signed-and-numbered limited edition of two hundred, was released through Upper Playground and sold out immediately. To celebrate Obama's electoral victory and for the inauguration, English, in the tradition of Andy Warhol, produced very limited editions of diamond-dust prints. Master printmaker Donald Sheridan, who printed Warhol's diamond-dust prints in the eighties, collaborated to produce three sets of 26x36-inch prints.

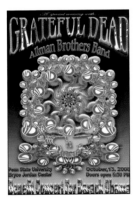

Curt Walters

Page 45: Curt Walters's poster for the Grateful Dead and the Allman Brothers concert at Penn State University on October 13, 2008, uses Indian religious iconography that instantly takes you back to those thrilling days of yesteryear at the Fillmore and Avalon Ballrooms—it reminds you of posters by the great Robert Fried, Victor Moscoso, Wes Wilson, Alton Kelley, and Stanley Mouse.

Wes Winship

Page 46, *top left:* This signed-and-numbered limited-edition screen print of three hundred was produced by Wes Winship for Change Rocks, two early-vote concerts held in North Carolina in 2008 featuring Arcade Fire and Superchunk. Previously, Winship had created a string of Superchunk screen prints, which made this one all the more desirable. This poster instantly won over North Carolinians, since the print portrays the famous lighthouses that dot the coast and then graphically recedes through the Piedmont and into the mountains.

Kristen Thiele

Page 46, *top right:* Friday night, May 2, in Carrboro, North Carolina, was a gig-poster-lover's dream come true. The Obama benefit concert not only featured what remained of the Wes Winship posters, it also featured this colorful and intriguing, signed-and-numbered limited-edition giclée poster created by Kristen Thiele, one of the top designers of rock concert posters. Growing up in Miami, Thiele ended up at the University of Miami on a full-ride scholarship. She then went off to graduate studies at the School of the Art Institute of Chicago, where she apprenticed with printmaker Steve Walters of Screwball Press. At Screwball Press she learned the art of screen-printing, producing posters for local and national bands. After returning to Florida, she now has a studio on South Beach in Miami where she continues to produce gig posters.

Change Rocks

Page 46, *bottom left:* Artists who performed for Obama in the Change Rocks series of concerts are numerous, and this is just one example of the dozens of posters that exist with the names of various artists in various locations. There are few large posters, most are no bigger than handbills, and it is likely that Obama for America used a digital master that they could quickly rearrange and into which they could plug changing or new information and then send out to the campaign headquarters of the city where the concert was to happen. It was up to the local headquarters if they wished to print out the digital files. This accounts for the variety, size, and paper quality of these very desirable gig announcements.

Alex Fine

Page 46, *bottom right:* While he was still in his teens in 1996, Alex Fine started creating posters for bands and clubs in the Baltimore and Washington, D.C., area, and he continues to do so. In 2004 he graduated from the Maryland Institute and College of Art. As a freelance artist/designer, he has done work for *ESPN: The Magazine*, *WWE Magazine*, *Philadelphia Weekly*, and *Phoenix Magazine*, to mention but a few. His favorite illustrators include Norman Rockwell, Charles Burns, and Yuko Shimizu. Poster artists he admires include Shepard Fairey, Coop, and Nolan Strals. Fine's Obama/Bruce Springsteen poster, done for a Philadelphia concert, proved very popular. People were attracted to his colorful images that capture the characters of his subjects in a kind of raw, exaggerated way.

Mickey Cuffe

Page 47, *top left:* Mickey Cuffe, explaining his birth and childhood, says he "entered the world through his parent's Jersey Bar ice cream shoppe in Utica, Illinois. Lulled to sleep by a slurpee machine as a baby, he is now unable to sleep without . . . some element of noise." He comes from a long line of European artists, and he continued the tradition by graduating from Marymount University in film and television production. A prolific sketch artist, he was influenced by the Brothers Hildebrandt, Edward Hopper, René Magritte, and Andy Warhol. Working in Hollywood painting murals and sets for cheap horror movies burned him out quickly, and he fled to San Francisco to pursue art. *The Hopeful Hearts Club*, a Beatles Sgt. Pepper takeoff, is a fun, retro, signed-and-numbered limited, offset edition of three thousand. Everybody seems to be in this picture, maybe even Waldo if you look hard enough.

Shepard Fairey

Page 47, *top right:* Almost as popular as *Hope,* this wonderfully designed retro poster for Rock the Vote was released in three sequences. The first 200 signed-and-numbered limited-edition screen prints of a run of 350 were offered through Shepard Fairey's website Obey Giant. The remaining 150 were sold framed for $250 by Rock the Vote as fundraisers. A later signed screen print that added "Democratic National Convention 2008, Denver, Colorado" at the bottom was sold in Denver. Rock the Vote is a left-of-center political organization whose purpose is to increase voter turnout among the young through music, popular culture, and new technologies.

Jeffrey Everett

Page 47: *(bottom)* Jeffrey Everett of El Jefe Design claims to be a failed rock star residing outside the nation's capital. His work has appeared in magazines like *Print, How,* and *Step Inside Design.* He has won silver and gold awards from the Art Directors Club and has produced everything from gig posters to works that have appeared in high-end galleries. Occasionally called to the hallowed halls of academia, he has also lectured at American University and the University of Baltimore. Everett combines many elements into his designs to meet clients' demands, but he says, "El Jefe always delivers the heavyweight designs." *Backin' Barack,* with its AC/DC look, was printed on recycled paper and released in a signed-and-numbered limited edition of one hundred.

Shepard Fairey

Page 48: *Change* is the first print from the *Artists for Obama* series and was released in a numbered edition of five thousand, of which the first two hundred were signed and mostly shipped to Illinois and Delaware delegates and a few select VIPs. Notice that Fairey pulled the candidate's head down and moved away from the harder lines to produce a less constructivist poster. Critics of *Hope,* many in the Democratic Party, maintained that the Communist revolutionary style Fairey was taken with made Obama look like a dictator pushing the cult of personality.

Shepard Fairey

Page 49: As Shepard Fairey's fame increased, so did his print runs, and they raised large amounts of money for the Obama campaign quickly. *Yes We Did* was created for MoveOn.org to commemorate Obama's landside victory in a numbered, limited edition of five thousand, of which the first one thousand were signed.

Pablo Serrano

Page 51: Pablo Serrano lives and works in the active art community developing in the Pilsen neighborhood of Chicago. Once mostly inhabited by Czech immigrants, it is now a mixed community with a predominance of Latinos. He incorporates elements associated with magical realism by utilizing traditional colorful images from artifacts used in Day of the Dead celebrations and in Mexican folk culture, as well as from the Aztec and Mayan past. *Democracy=Change* is a signed, giclée, limited edition.

DEMOCRACY = CHANGE

Joseph Griffith

Page 52: Hawaiian cartoon character Obama rides the inside of the curl of this huge wave—a tsunami of change. The wave is appropriated from the famous Japanese woodblock print artist Hokusai's *Thirty-Six Views of Mount Fuji.* You have to love this one.

WAVE OF HOPE
JOSEPH GRIFFITH

Patrick Moberg

Page 53: When Patrick Moberg finished his design of the forty-four presidents and an Obama portrait, he received licensing offers, but he decided that if he wanted quality prints, he would have to print them himself. He zipped around New York to find the appropriate paper and screen-printed and dried his Obama portrait in his tiny apartment. *Today Is a Big Day,* the title for the forty-four presidents image, is a signed, open-edition giclée print also likely run off in Patrick's apartment.

Robbie Conal

Page 54: Robbie Conal grew up in New York City, but according to Smart Art Press he was an early immigrant to the Haight-Ashbury neighborhood in San Francisco in 1964, three years before the "Summer of Love." In Los Angeles he began his art attacks on the streets of the city, helping to pioneer the agitprop/guerrilla/graffiti street art movement. *LA Weekly* now provides the outlet for Conal's caricatures satirizing politicians, TV's talking heads, televangelists, the rich, the famous, the mighty, and the self-important. He has established himself as an important poster maker, and his work has appeared in numerous newspapers and magazines. In 1992 he published *Art Attack: The Midnight Politics of a Guerilla Artist.* In 2004, along with Shepard Fairey and "Mear One," he undertook an agitprop anti-Bush guerrilla street campaign called Be the Revolution.

CLIMATE CHANGE

Felix Jackson

Page 55: Born on a naval base in Norfolk, Virginia, Felix Jackson graduated from Florida State University in 2006 and then moved to Denver, where he says he is always cold. His work, he says, "stems from watching way too much television, bright moments, and sparse memories of his grandma's house." *Yes, Please* is a signed-and-numbered limited-edition screen print.

Scott Hansen

Page 56: Scott Hansen is a well-known West Coast artist and musician who created *Progress*, the second poster in the series *Artists for Obama*, on his computer. The resulting giclée was printed on a very large press from a monster-size graphics file. The 23x40-inch poster, printed on heavy stock, ate up 2.77 gigabytes and included over one thousand layers. Hansen states that he likes to avoid trendy changes and concentrate on looking back. For him, that looking back focuses on the height of the Bauhaus movement in Europe and in America in the 1960s. His goal is to create something beautiful that taps into the roots of visual communication and expresses those concepts in an understandable form. "When I see something that embodies these ideals it is always very moving, these are the things that drive me to create."

Zak Kaplan

Page 57: Born in Washington, D.C., in 1977, Zak Kaplan grew up in central New Jersey. A high school art major, he learned guitar and later ended up playing in a number of punk bands in New Brunswick, a college town with a booming music scene. Days found Kaplan learning documentary photography as a visual arts major in the Mason Gross School of Art, Rutgers University. Just before graduation, Kaplan dropped in to see an art show of Russian constructivists and other Soviet propaganda artists. He had an epiphany, and it became a passion shared by fellow artist Shepard Fairey. Kaplan plunged pell-mell into graphic design and mastered design software. In Ashbury, he went to work as a designer for the New Jersey Punk Pioneers. Presently, Kaplan's company, Rogue State Design in Allentown, Pennsylvania, has a wide variety of clients. He continues to turn out gig posters.

Antar Dayal

Page 58: Antar Dayal, a longtime Santa Barbara printmaker, created this one-of-a-kind giclée print, *Obama: Yes We Can*, at the invitation of the Obama campaign, but it was initially rejected. Dayal went back to work and produced a print more to the campaign's liking. Dayal recalls when he was a poor, young, free spirit in Paris but always found the money for admission to the Louvre, where Delacroix's *Liberty Leading the People* brought him to the realization that he was "not only going to paint nice and beautiful things." His art would demand a commitment to history, to interpreting the past honestly, and to preserving "my impressions about life and events during my own lifetime, even if I would not at the moment understand the full extent or even the tragedy of it."

Dustin Parker

Page 59: Dustin Parker is a painter, video artist, and graphic designer living and working in Wichita, Kansas. A graduate in art from Friends University, he is the founder, editor, and art director of *Proteus Magazine*, an online forum for art and design. He has had several one-man shows and has been included in a long list of group art shows. *Hope, Freedom, Change, Progress* is a signed, open-edition giclée print available in two sizes, 8x10-inch and 16x20-inch.

Kishore Nallan

Page 60: Demonstrating the global nature of the new rising art movement is the work of Kishore Nallan, who resides in Chennai, India, and produced this signed, open-edition print on handmade cotton paper using an old platen letterpress. Obama's portrait is constructed solely of typeface from a number of font families. Nallan is excited about his letterpress work and strives to gain recognition for and acceptance of this venerable printing process.

Branden Otto

Page 61: When the Obama fundraising concert gig posters that announced the October 13, 2008, Penn State University performance by the Deadheads and Allman Brothers Band failed to arrive, Branden Otto quickly grabbed a pencil and drew this winning portrait of the future president. Most of these posters, printed in this signed and numbered giclée edition of twenty, saw service on campus.

Mr. Brainwash

Page 62: Mr. Brainwash (who signs his work "MBW") has spent the better part of a decade filming street art for the ultimate documentary on these stealthy nighttime guerrilla art actions. Along the way, however, he became seduced by the process he was witnessing and became a participant. He started with small hand-drawn stickers and then moved up to big prints—really big, like billboards. His use of current pop cultural icons is in a style much like that of Andy Warhol. His *Marilyn Obama*, Obama in a blonde wig with lipstick and looking surprisingly like Marilyn Monroe, is hilarious. MBW's portrait of Obama as Superman, standing in front of the American flag, looking defiant and above the fray, is set off in a traditional gold frame. The utter incongruity of the piece gives it its charm. The print was released in a signed-and-numbered limited edition of three hundred.

Paul Friedrich

Page 63: Paul Friedrich was nominated for the Eisner Award for his creation of the comic strip *Onion Head*. He is known for his bold use of color and the inclusion of humor in his artwork. He is the co-founder of SparkCon, one of the South's preeminent conferences on creativity. Also a member of the award-winning DesignBox, he recently painted a graffiti mural at the new Marbles Kids Museum. Editor of *HellCar* magazine, he is also the author/illustrator of three books, *Lion!*, *Don't Trust Evel Knievel*, and *The Boy Who Cried Wolf*. Friedrich did a small drawing for his Obama poster, fed it into the computer, and produced this brooding red and black giclée poster that calls to mind the fabulous woodcuts done by early German expressionists.

Mason Fetzer

Page 65, *top left:* Mason Fetzer was born in Salt Lake City, Utah, in 1982. He graduated from the University of Utah in 2006 with a degree in painting and drawing. He spent two years in pre-med studying biology and anatomy, where he learned to love the scalpel. Slowly the realization dawned on him that medicine was not his calling—it was art. Fetzer now runs his own freelance company and uses an X-Acto knife with the same passion with which he wielded the scalpel. *We Need Hope* is an open-edition giclée print.

Mason Fetzer

Page 65, *top right:* Mason Fetzer says that once on a family vacation, "I noticed out the window of our family van that the mountains pass by slower than the fences; the fences go by slower than the road. I am fascinated by the physiology of this visual depth of field. Later, I am back home and playing Nintendo, I notice as I play that the mountains go by slower than the fences, the fences go by slower than the road." In *We Need Peace*, an open-edition giclée print, Fetzer attempts to re-create the effects of his observation.

Mason Fetzer

Page 65, *bottom left: We Need Change*, like much of Mason Fetzer's work, demonstrates his commitment to precision, to the computer, and to the layering that modern software packages make possible.

Mason Fetzer

Page 65, *bottom right:* After a day of spray-painting large-scale graffiti murals and hand-painted portraits on commission, Mason Fetzer relaxes by singing and playing lead guitar in his band, Precinct. *We One* was painted to celebrate Obama's election victory and is a signed-and-numbered limited-edition giclée print in a run of thirty.

Ray Noland

Page 66: *First* was designed by Ray Noland to commemorate Obama's November 4, 2008, election victory in a signed-and-numbered limited-edition screen print of 250. A black American had become president of the United States. For many people, this reality, the dream fulfilled, sank in very slowly. On victory night in Grant Park, when Obama spoke to the crowd, Noland was overcome with emotion. His incredible efforts and those of others had paid off.

Ray Noland

Page 67: With the printing of *First*, featuring Michelle Obama, Ray Noland produced a fine screen-print diptych in a signed-and-numbered limited edition of one hundred. First and first: America would have a black American woman as first lady.

Brian Campbell

Page 68: For a number of years, Brian Campbell has designed and manufactured campaign buttons in limited editions that have sold well and are valued by collectors. *Reject Propaganda* is his first venture into political poster art, and he was obviously influenced by Roy Lichtenstein and the 1960s Pop Artists. Campbell says he was moved to create a poster that was not simply a photograph manipulated in a computer graphic software package and did not look like a Shepard Fairey. He also says, "the cartoon image and the Obama image were painted with acrylic paint by hand." The run consists of one hundred signed-and-numbered glossy-finish giclée prints.

Leia Bell

Page 69: Leia Bell grew up in Tennessee, and as a young girl, she sold her drawings door to door. She saved nothing, however, and instead spent her money on Pop Rocks and Pixy Stix. Undecided about art, even after her successful ventures as a child, she nevertheless attended the University of Utah to study photography and printmaking. After graduating, Bell was not sure how to put her art degree to work until Phil, the owner of Kirby Court (a rock venue), thought she might create some screen-print gig posters, posters that would appeal to collectors as well as to rockers. She took Phil's advice, and the posters were a success. Bell has since produced dozens and dozens of posters, married Phil, had three boys, adopted two dogs and a cat, and has begun working in a print studio and a woodshop. Her print, *Barack*, is a signed-and-numbered limited-edition screen print of 120.

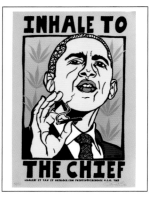

Jon-Paul Bail

Page 70: Perhaps the most controversial of all the Obama posters, Jon-Paul Bail's now infamous *Inhale to the Chief* can be seen plastered up around Oakland, California. It has stirred up a hornet's nest of discussion and criticism, particularly among those with little sense of humor. First issued as an open, offset edition, Bail also created a signed, numbered screen print, using gold ink for Obama's face, in an edition of 150.

Mear One

Page 71: Growing up in Santa Cruz, California, "Mear One" (Kalen Ockerman) started as a graffiti street artist. He is often referred to as the "Michelangelo" of graffiti. In 2004 he partnered with Shepard Fairey and Robbie Conal in an anti-Bush agitprop guerrilla street campaign entitled Be the Revolution. Politics run deep in his work, and his goal is to have his paintings "see through the illusion of our decrepit social condition and speak out with art as a weapon of mass liberation." Mear One maintains that the quest of his life is to be a messenger, a spiritual warrior. His Obama print was a part of the series released through Upper Playground in a signed-and-numbered limited edition of fifty.

Russell Baltes

Page 72: Entitled *Obama Arcade Lettering*, this hot, open-edition poster was distributed by the website Democratic Stuff, which manufactures its products through Tigereye Design. While Tigereye makes mostly democratic stuff, the company also does custom work for several political groups, as well as for businesses throughout the country. The company got its start making campaign buttons and then just continued to grow. The artist is Russell Baltes.

Russell Baltes

Page 73: Entitled *Obama Retro Lettering*, this open-edition poster was also offered by Democratic Stuff and designed by Russell Baltes. "Being a part of the design movement was as important for me as it was to be part of the political process," Baltes says. "An unprecedented attention to art and design was so thrilling to witness as a public awareness was formed." Tigereye Design, located on the edge of Greenville, Ohio, is a union company and largely a supplier of all types of union paraphernalia, including a clothing line.

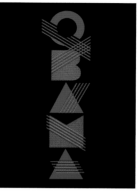

Mags

Page 75, *top left:* "Mags" (Margaret Coble) is a New Orleans artist and electronic music magazine editor who has turned out her Obama stencil prints by the hundreds in two-color and in one-of-a-kind artist proofs. Fusing politics with arts and crafts, she calls herself an "art-n-craftivist" and her work has been influenced by the 1960s pop movement, urban street art, graphic and commercial art, and folk art from around the world. Combining stenciling with found objects is one of her favorite ways to work. *Believe* is a spray-paint stencil in a signed and numbered edition.

Ray Noland

Page 75, *top right: The Dream* was Ray Noland's first Obama presidential campaign poster, one circulated to friends on the Internet who reported back, "great Ray, go for it." Noland printed this striking mustard-yellow poster, with Obama's head surrounded by a nimbus reminiscent of a Russian icon or Catholic Church idolatry, in a signed-and-numbered limited-edition screen print of sixty. The print sold rapidly; viewers became attached to this saintly portrayal of their candidate. Encouraged, Noland plunged into his officially unofficial one-man Obama campaign. Money from *The Dream* was used to produce cheaper, offset street posters of his newer creations. Noland later printed *The Dream* in a second signed-and-numbered limited edition of sixty and an unsigned edition on heavy stock paper.

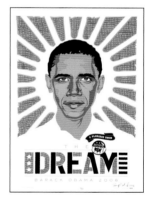

Jason Krekel

Page 75, *bottom left:* Jason Krekel comes from a talented family. His father, Tim Krekel, wrote hit songs for two of country music's biggest stars—Crystal Gail and Patti Lovelace—and was a session guitarist for Jimmy Buffet's Coral Reefer Band. Jason Krekel spent his early years in Nashville learning to play multiple instruments, and he played with an assortment of bands from 1995 to 2000—bands like Snake Oil Medicine, Cygnus-X-1, Blackhole, Bluegrass Boyz, and the Larry Keel Experience. On the art side, he joined Handcranked letterpress and designed the posters and graphic materials for the Firecracker Jazz Band and Mad Tea Party, bands in which he also plays. He cranked out three Obama letterpress prints, one in a signed-and-numbered limited edition of fifty, and two others in open editions.

Unknown artist

Page 75, *bottom right:* This giclée Obama poster appeared in installations in numerous locations in Seattle, Washington. To date, no one seems to know who the artist is. The secret phantom of Seattle, a true guerrilla street artist, has managed to maintain his anonymity and foreswear fame and fortune.

Thomas Brodahl

Page 76: A well-known web designer and computer artist who is greatly influenced by classical Bauhaus designs, Thomas Brodahl used red and green circles and triangles to form the letters under his Obama portraits. When he was ten years old, Brodahl moved from Bergen, Norway, to Luxembourg and graduated from the American International School in 1996. At the University of Virginia, he took a course in HTML 3, fell in love with web design, left the university, and returned to Luxembourg, where he started his own design studio. He founded the online design magazine *Surfstation.lu*, which proved very successful. In 2004 he moved to Los Angeles, partnered with Jessy Cinis, and started Stolen Inc. to produce a line of T-shirts. Like Barack Obama, he loves the game of basketball and plays as often as possible.

Zoltron

Page 77: For those who could not afford the nearly endless run of signed limited editions being printed during the Obama campaign, the sticker, rabidly collected, became the poor man's print. As a committed member of the sticker revolution and creator of Sticker Robot, Zoltron produced a great many featuring his own designs. *Obama*, also available in a blue design, mimics retro movie poster style. The popularity of this design enticed Zoltron to create a signed-and-numbered giclée limited edition of one hundred.

Gui Borchert

Page 78: On close inspection, the Gui Borchert poster from the *Artists for Obama* series (printed in a numbered edition of five thousand) is an amazing piece of work: The Obama portrait is made up of twenty thousand words from the candidate's speeches. Borchert was recently named one of the top twenty designers under thirty years old by *Print* magazine. He is also one of the top creative designers for the Nike line of shoes and apparel.

Bask

Page 79: Alex Hostomsky, who goes by the nickname "Bask," moved to Florida with his parents from the Czech Republic. As a teenager he was especially interested in American advertising imagery and thought there was very little difference between the Communist propaganda of his childhood and the popular culture imagery that daily bombarded Americans. Deciding that he was being manipulated, even controlled, he looked carefully into advertising propaganda and discovered conspiracies. He began to paint the decay and the debris that is everywhere in cities and to deplore a consumer society devoid of meaning. The modern world eats its own tail. His signed-and-numbered limited-edition screen print of two hundred points to a limited, tentative progress that is as hopeful as Bask can be.

Print Liberation

Page 80: The creators of Print Liberation, Jamie Dillon and Nick Paparone of Dayton, Ohio, describe the company through the following metaphor: "Let's say you have two options for lunch today. Here at Print Liberation, we think of ourselves as two guys running a sandwich shop. Everything that leaves our studio is printed and designed by us—fresh, delicious, and new." In a retro move, these two also have demonstrated a love of "floating heads," a popular graphic style found in Eisenhower/Nixon and Kennedy/Johnson posters. Their Obama "floating head print," an open-edition screen print based on a half-tone process that enlarges the dots, is top-notch. Moving beyond poster/printmaking, this dynamic duo has created logos, done photo shoots for magazines, and spearheaded full print campaigns for sneakers, car shares, museums, and commercial space.

Matt Dye

Page 81: Influenced by a punk rock aesthetic, which appealed to a generation of disaffected young people looking to shock the world out of its slumber, Matt Dye's Obama prints can be outrageous and humorous in varying degrees, depending on the observer's own perspective. One of the best and quintessential examples of this artistic shock value is *Obama Extended*, which confronts the fears of an assassination head-on, at least mythically. A 007 Bond–like or Clint Eastwood–like Obama, a Superfly Obama, clinched cigarette in teeth, stands behind the image of a "pimped out" 1963 Kennedy assassination limousine pointing a huge gun at anyone foolish enough to attempt the evil deed. This screen print is a signed, open edition.

Stephen Fowler

Page 82: Stephen Fowler founded Gemini Studio Art with his twin brother, Ryan, in 1998. The twins grew up in Ohio, moved occasionally, and eventually settled in the Lakeview neighborhood of Chicago. At first, Gemini turned out handmade greeting cards, but it since has expanded to include graphic design, commercial art, illustration, and photography. *Yes We Can* was printed in a signed-and-numbered limited edition of fifty.

Stephen Fowler

Page 83: In formulating his pieces, Stephen Fowler collages high-quality prints of his own artwork onto canvases. Applying glue sealer and other materials, he is able to create textured layers that make for one-of-kind graphic art pieces. *Hope*, in a signed-and-numbered limited edition of fifty, is a giclée print.

Lance Wyman

Page 84: As a young designer, Lance Wyman made his reputation branding the 1968 Mexico Olympics with simple, high-impact designs. He designed the signage for the 1970 Mexico Soccer World Cup and the directional signage for the Mexico City Metro. In fact, this poster in the *Artists for Obama* series—released in a numbered, limited edition of five thousand in red, white, and blue—is reminiscent of the Olympic logo with its very effective use of minimalist repetition. Wyman has written widely on the principles of graphic design and here attempts to capture Obama's rhetorical skills as a communicator.

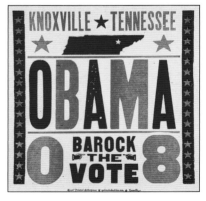

Scot Lefavor

Page 85: Raised a South Bostonian, Scot Lefavor attended the Hartford Art School, studying under design professors Mark Snyder and Nancy Wynn and printmakers Fred Wessel and John Willis before he took seriously the advice of Horace Greeley and moved west to Colorado. Colorado held career opportunities and, as important, the possibility of incredible snowboarding during the endless winter. In Boulder, Lefavor jumped into the art scene and from 2002 to 2004 co-owned the Gallery Sovereign. As a freelancer, he designed websites and took design commissions and began to explore the close interchange between printmaking and painting through the use of acrylic paint, spray paint, screen-printing, gel transfers, and enamel. Influenced by street art and the 1960s Pop Art movement, his narrative work is strongly rooted in traditional sign painting and typography.

Kevin Bradley

Page 86: Kevin Bradley, born in the Davy Crockett backwoods country of Tennessee, began to learn printmaking, graphic design, and painting while he was a student at the University of Tennessee and decided, rightly, that the computer was the devil. He soon met Julie Belcher, with whom he shared similar interests, and they partnered to found Yee Haw Industries, dedicated to continuing and reviving the art of the letterpress. From Kansas City (Hammer Press) to Nashville (Hatch Show Print) to Knoxville (Yee Haw Industries) and over the big mountain to Ashville (Handcranked), letterpress has flourished. Bradley's limited-edition Johnny Cash and Woody Guthrie prints are wonderfully rendered and have a rough, country, woodblock quality with a hint of German expressionism that is very appealing.

Antar Dayal

Page 87: *Yes We Can* met with approval from the Obama campaign and took its place as the third print in the *Artists for Obama* series. In a run of five thousand numbered prints, the first two hundred were signed as well and were gifts to big contributors, VIPs, and Illinois and Delaware delegates. Antar Dayal created the image on his Kaolin-coated scratchboard. He then coated the image with black China ink and engraved the fine lines "into the surface, sculpting shadows and highlights."

Christopher Cox

Page 88: In 2002, Denver-based Chris Cox started a blog called Changethethought that discussed design principles and their application. Also on the website was an Obama section that included a wide variety of Obama campaign material. All available as free downloads, there were posters, stickers, and buttons galore. Just before Obama clinched the nomination, Cox decided to create what he called a "commemorative poster." He wanted his poster to be "more ageless and less trendy—something older voters would appreciate . . . something they could hang on their wall." Like Scott Hansen's *Progress* print, this monster giclée ate up nearly three gigabytes of space. Cox used the Obama campaign's favorite typeface—Gotham—and he printed the poster on white 100-stock paper in order to preserve the highlight effect on Obama's face.

Robert Indiana

Page 89: Robert Indiana was born in New Castle, Indiana. After high school, he studied at the School of the Art Institute of Chicago. His classmates included the now-famous pop artist Claes Oldenburg and the realist photographer Richard Estes. Indiana's posters abound, and his work is in over one hundred museums worldwide. His sculpture, *Hope*, was unveiled at the Democratic National Convention in Denver. In the *Artists for Obama* series, his Hope poster, a reworking of his hugely iconic *Love* design, was issued in a signed-and-numbered limited-edition screen print of two hundred that sold out at the whopping price of $2,500 each.

Vonda Sisneros

Page 90: Vonda Sisneros, Denver-based, is the queen of American sports art, having painted hundreds of star athletes in dozens of sports. She has an art degree from Colorado State University, and she worked for a number of years in art education. She and her husband run Authentic Sports Art, an autograph and sports painting business for which their work is largely commissioned by professional athletes. Her *Obama 2008* was commissioned by the Democratic National Committee.

Anthony Armstrong

Page 91: When growing up in Georgia, Anthony Armstrong was encouraged to draw, so he more closely observed the things around him. Today, working in his Atlanta studio, he is influenced by recollections of the past, stories told to him by his mother, and his religious inspiration, all of which provide a rich storehouse for his imagination. Armstrong has been extremely productive the last few years. He calls it "a flurry of excitement" revolving around "what I am, my faith in God, pride in my race, and my love of beauty."

Jon-Paul Bail

Page 92: Jon-Paul Bail, who has been conducting anti-Bush guerrilla street art actions for a number of years, finally dropped in, at least for the moment, to support Obama. All of Bail's work emanating from his Gridlock Studio pushes the envelope, and *Clean* is no exception. His Bush, McCain, and Palin posters, plastered to the side of an Oakland building tagged the wall of shame, use a sickly green color for all three faces that is reminiscent of the powerful Andy Warhol *Vote McGovern '72*. Bail is dedicated to the making of hand-crafted prints as a method of visual protest.

deedee9:14

Page 93: Dee Adams ("deedee9:14"), whose pseudonym comes from her birthday, September 14, has been fascinated since her early childhood with the arrangement of colors, accentuated by a Josef Albers print that hung on her parents' wall. Adams recalls that this "singular piece held everything for me . . . the simplicity of shape, color, line." The same print hanging on her wall today "continually influences everything" she creates. Adams is a color field painter influenced by, among others, Gustav Klimt and Mondrian. Her Andy Warhol–like Obama giclée print adorned billboards in Times Square and in San Francisco, treating passersby to her vibrant use of color.

Caleb Halter

Page 94: At age two, Caleb Halter spent much of his time at the family table drawing. Of course, he grew up and went to art school. He now works as a motion graphics designer for Lightborne in Cincinnati. One look at this poster, and the knowledgeable viewer knows full well that Halter has been heavily influenced by classic Bauhaus design. This was produced for an Ohio early vote concert in an open, offset edition, and the concert turned out over two thousand potential voters. The poster was an instant hit. Event sponsors showed the poster to candidate Obama, who remarked, "Wow . . . that's cool."

Eileen Burke

Page 95: Eileen Burke, inspired by Obama's uplifting messages, created this signed-and-numbered limited-edition giclée print in a run of three hundred. Overlaying the words from Obama's New Hampshire primary speech, the first time he uttered "yes, we can," is a silhouetted Obama, microphone in hand under the moon. Looking back she says that she was "born into a pale Irish family and raised working in the family restaurant surrounded by creative types stuck waiting tables." She studied at three colleges, thousands of bookstores, and hundreds of museums in far-flung corners of the world. "Typography is everywhere, and I collect it all with sketches and photographs. Wherever there's organic shape, color, texture, I see the seed of a new design. The world is my visual thesaurus, and I'm always seeking just the right element to communicate a message clearly."

Mario Torero

Page 97: Mario Torero is a well-known figure in San Diego, with his huge outdoor murals dotting the city. A longtime activist, in the 1960s he plunged into the Chicano movement to preserve Chicano Park partly by painting murals. *El Movemiento* succeeded in improving the neighborhood by getting rid of drugs and cleaning up the trash. In 1986, he painted a mural that included Martin Luther King Jr., César Chávez, and Mahatma Gandhi and recently restored the work to help preserve a piece of African-American heritage. Back in Chicano Park, Torero started an all-day Saturday art school that also undertakes park improvement projects. Strong-willed and committed, he fought to preserve a downtown San Diego mural he called *Eyes of Picasso* and eventually prevailed after repainting it twice on two different buildings. His highly charged political murals are in the tradition of Diego Rivera. His *Obama* print is a signed giclée.

Emmanuelle Fevre

Page 98: Emmanuelle Fevre originally designed one poster, *Yes We Can*, for the Paris, France, art show at Dorothy's Gallery entitled Barack in Paris and scheduled to run from October 3 to November 17, 2008. Over twenty artists expressed their support of Obama with original artwork. Owner Dorothy Polley stated she was dedicating the gallery to Barack Obama, his life, ideas, and vision of the future. The show was sponsored by Zachary Miller, the co-chair of Democrats Abroad France, and Sol Solvit, president of the French Committee for Obama. The exhibition proved so popular that it was extended into February 2009.

The Date Farmers

Page 99: Marsea Goldberg of New Image Art gave these young artists their first show and tagged Armando Lerma and Carlos Ramirez "the Date Farmers," since Armando's father owned a date farm in Coachella, California, and Carlos had worked there picking dates. Deep roots in the Mexican-American agricultural communities of Southern California have influenced their work, as have pop art and the work of Mexican artist Jose Guadalupe Posada. Their collages and paintings include found objects and elements of graffiti, Mexican street murals, revolutionary posters, sign painting, prison art, and tattoos. As part of the Upper Playground print series, *Si Se Puede* was released in a signed and numbered, limited-edition screen print of three hundred.

Rafael Lopez

Page 100: Growing up in Mexico City, the son of architects and teachers, Rafael Lopez was strongly influenced by the Latin American tradition of magical symbolism or magical realism in art and literature. The paintings of Frida Kahlo and the writings of Gabriel Garcia Marquez come to mind. His use of vibrant color to portray children and capture everyday street life in paintings and children's books is a testament, as Carlos Fuentes remarked, to the "fusing of myth and fact, dreams and vigil, reason and fantasy," on a daily basis in people's lives throughout Latin America. *Voz Unida* (*One Voice*), in the *Artists for Obama* series, is a numbered, limited edition of one thousand.

Eddie

Page 101: All of the posters in this series have been criticized for making Obama look dictatorial and for being far too much like posters made for Stalin, Ho Chi Minh, Kim Jong-il, Fidel Castro, and Mao Zedong. With the large Chinese characters for "forward" on the bottom of the poster, it is hard not to acknowledge the comparison, especially with Mao. An older Chinese friend once commented that when he saw this poster in San Francisco, he had to pinch himself to be sure where he was. Many a Chinese poster from the Red Guard days used the rays of the sun to glorify the great leader on the nation's march forward. Given the history of this poster style, proponents and opponents alike recognize the power and effectiveness of these attention-getting posters.

Justin Bua

Page 102: Justin Bua created his hard-edged Obama portrait, *One*, for Upper Playground in a signed-and-numbered limited edition of two hundred. His style, called "distorted urban realism," captures the pain of the city's underside and yet celebrates its vibrancy. Favorite subjects of his include hip-hop and jazz musicians. Raised by a single mom and growing up on the Upper West Side of New York City, he was positioned to watch and participate in the street life at Rock Steady Park and in the Douglas projects. Attending the High School of Music and Performing Arts, Bua moved into break-dancing performance with the New York Express and the Dynamic Breakers. After graduating from the Art Center College of Design in Pasadena, he started as a slick-bottom painter for a skateboard company but went on to produce a series of posters and to design CD covers. His striking urban street scenes are reminiscent of Reginald Marsh and Ben Shahn.

Benjamin Kuehn

Page 103: An intriguing aspect of this poster is that the rust-red portrait of Obama is overprinted on a background of small Obama logos that form a star. Benjamin Kuehn printed this poster, *Change Obama '08*, in two sizes, and he printed a blue and white version also in two sizes. All four posters were in signed-and-numbered limited editions of seventy-five.

Billi Kid

Page 105: Born in Columbia, Billi Kid resides in Darien, Connecticut, and works in New York City. In 1987 he received a BFA degree from Parsons The New School for Design. He maintains that he is determined to find his voice in the "oversaturated global and cyber landscapes." Since childhood he has been a doodler as well as an art lover and design enthusiast. His work, he says, "blurs the lines between graffiti, pop culture, and art." An innovative street artist immersed in "sticker culture," Billi Kid constructed eye-popping Obama sticker collages, often around Zoltron posters, in New York City and surrounding communities during the campaign. Kid also produced a number of Barack Obama and Michelle Obama screen prints, as well as using stencils to create spray-painted pieces on wood panels. This print is a signed edition.

Steve Lowtwait

Page 106: Steve Lowtwait, who resides in Boulder, Colorado, is a self-employed artist. For a number of years he created posters for the Colorado travel and sky industry. Inspired by Obama's candidacy, Lowtwait decided to design a poster and to create an array of Obama paraphernalia, then during the Democratic National Convention he spent the week outside the convention hall selling the items he had designed and made. *Progress* is an open, signed edition.

Guy Juke

Page 107: Artist Guy Juke's career highlights include handbills for Butch Hancock and gig posters for Asleep at the Wheel, the Terry and Jo Harvey Allen Band, and Jerry Jeff Walker, among many others. His screen prints and recent designs for Kinky Friedman's Texas gubernatorial campaign are also avidly sought by collectors. This maroon *Compassion for a Change* screen print is a signed-and-numbered edition.

Mr. Brainwash

Page 108: Often outrageous, Mr. Brainwash, a Los Angeles artist and eccentric French filmmaker, used the fight venue for his *McCain vs. Obama* print, a signed-and-numbered limited-edition screen print in a run of three hundred. A desirable quality of Mr. Brainwash posters is that they are printed on heavy paper in a large format.

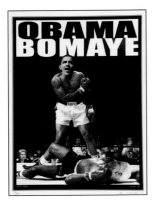

EMEK

Page 109: Born in Israel in 1970, Emek Golan and his family later immigrated to the United States. In the 1990s, he began creating rock concert posters. The *Portland Oregonian* maintains that Golan was a "savior of rock 'n' roll. Not the music, but the art." Golan discovered that one of Obama's favorite photos features Mohammed Ali knocking out George Foreman in the famous "rumble in the jungle" in Kinshasa, Zaire, October 30, 1974. The title of Golan's poster is *Obama Bomaye*, a play on the slogan chanted by thousands of jubilant Ali supporters, "Ali Bomaye," before, during, and after the match. In the African French dialect spoken in Zaire, "Obama Bomaye" means "Obama, kill him." Hillary Clinton watches from the lower left-hand corner of this special, signed-and-numbered limited-edition print. Golan would later add the image of Joe Biden to the right of Hillary, and that of George W. Bush, Sarah Palin, and Karl Rove in the lower right-hand corner.

Alex Ross

Page 110: Alex Ross was born into an artistic family in Lubbock, Texas. As a young man who loved to draw, he soon discovered Spider-Man, a colorful hero who defended the weak, took on the "bad guys," and protected the nation. When Ross discovered the photorealistic style of great illustrators like Andrew Loomis and Norman Rockwell, he set out to incorporate photorealism into comic books. At the American Academy of Art in Chicago, he studied classic illustrators like C. Leyendecker and was greatly influenced by the work of Salvador Dali. He also admires comic book artists George Perez and Berni Wrightson. As Ross progressed in his career, Kurt Busiak at Marvel Comics suggested a collaborative project that resulted in a graphic novel entitled *Marvels*—a panoply of superheroes. Soon after, Ross began painting tabloid-size books of Superman, Batman, Captain Marvel, and Wonder Woman. *Super Obama* is a giclée, signed and numbered edition.

Official Obama Campaign

Page 111: The Obama for America design team produced this effective poster, *Change We Can Believe In,* for the hotly contested South Carolina primary. One of the great strengths of the members of the design team was their ability to focus graphically on particular states and particular targeted audiences.

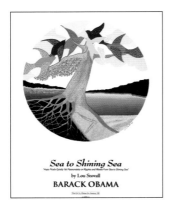

Lou Stovall

Page 112, *top:* An outstanding African-American artist and printmaker, Lou Stovall grew up in Springfield, Massachusetts, and later attended the Rhode Island School of Design and Howard University. As an ardent nature supporter with deep agrarian roots, he recognizes the fragility of the earth and its need for stewardship, and because of this, nature is a theme that he returns to over and over again. While working in his studio, Stovall plays the music of Rachmaninoff and other favorite composers at deafening decibels, maintaining that music interacts with nature to produce a more unified landscape. This poster, in a limited edition of one thousand, utilizes the design he did for *Artists for Obama.*

Lou Stovall

Page 112, *bottom:* Lou Stovall spends a good deal of time selecting the colors he wishes to use, a process he calls "accessorizing," and the success of that endeavor is clearly seen in his *Obama/Biden* signed and numbered screen-print edition of 140. As a master printer, he has worked with other famous artists like Josef Albers, Peter Blume, Alexander Calder, Elizabeth Catlett, Gene Davis, David Driskell, Sam Gilliam, Lois Mailou Jones, Jacob Lawrence, Robert Mangold, Mathieu Mategot, A. Brockie Stevenson, and James L. Wells.

Lindsey Kuhn

Page 113: While in high school in Mississippi, Lindsey Kuhn began designing and making gig flyers for punk shows and skateboarding events. Leaving Mississippi behind, Kuhn attended the University of South Alabama and then fled to Austin, Texas, a thriving center of music and poster makers. His job, however, was boring and seemingly endless; he worked for a sweatshop T-shirt operation where he screen-printed thirteen thousand shirts a day. Escaping the grind, he attended the Austin Record Convention, where he met Debbie Jacobson (owner of the L'Imagerie Gallery), who offered him a job. He thankfully took it and soon had printed posters for a number of poster luminaries like Frank Kozik, Robert Crumb, the Pizz, and Big Daddy Roth. Today, Kuhn owes his own business, SWAMP, and claims he "will screen anything and everything." His electric-acid *Obama 2008* print is a signed and numbered edition of ninety-nine.

Justin Hampton

Page 114: In 1990 Justin Hampton went to work for two of Seattle's prestigious designers, Art Chantry and Jeff Kleinsmith at *Rocket* magazine. Almost twenty years later, he has an independent business, and his rock posters are world famous. He was born and grew up in Santa Cruz, where he was influenced by street art, skate punk, and comic book artists like Jack Kirby and Mike Mignola, as well as the creator of the modern poster, Henri de Toulouse-Lautrec. Hampton has screen-printed for rock luminaries like Radiohead, Nine Inch Nails, Pearl Jam, Bob Dylan, Nick Cave, and Queen of the Stone Age. His client list runs in the dozens. Currently he is working on a twelve-part graphic novel that retells the stories of the Grimm Brothers in modern New York.

Shepard Fairey

Page 115: *History in Denver 5280* graced the cover of the August issue of the popular Denver magazine *5280*. Offset prints of the poster were up in magazine shops, kiosks, and bookstores.

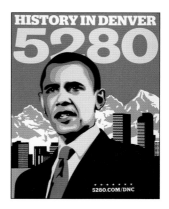

Ray Noland

Page 116, *top left:* This is a different take on what might be called Ray Noland's basketball series, but in this print the Obama logo is perfectly balanced against the gold background. Here, too, like with *Nothin' but Next*, Noland completely relies on nonverbal imagery.

Ray Noland

Page 116, *top right: Obama Balance*, a signed-and-numbered limited-edition screen print of fifty, refers to Obama's time teaching Constitutional law at the University of Chicago as well as to his time on the basketball court, a necessary coming together of two different worlds. When Ray Noland first decided Obama was the right candidate, he maintained that: "Excluding race, Obama was everything America would love in a political leader. The only thing that could possibly handicap him was the color of his skin. Would this country see beyond that; would it be okay if the answer to America's problems were black?"

Ray Noland

Page 116, *bottom left:* Created as a celebration of the inauguration of Barack Obama, forty-fourth president of the United States, this basketball jersey sports the number 44 and was printed in a signed-and-numbered limited edition of forty-four.

Ray Noland

Page 116, *bottom right:* Ray Noland was the first on the streets with Obama posters in the summer of 2007. The founding father of the Obama poster phenomenon, Noland began timidly. In the alleyway behind his house he pasted up *Coast to Coast* and *Street*. Ray's bold design, influenced by Russian constructivism that had been filtered through the direct colorful poster art of Saul Bass, hit the viewer in the gut like a smokin' basketball pass on the way to the jam. As Noland became more emboldened, *Coast to Coast* and *Street* popped up in carefully thought-out installations around Chicago. Signing his art "CRO, Creative Rescue Organization" Ray used anonymity and street artists' tactics to conduct stealthy nighttime guerilla operations that helped him avoid discovery and arrest. These tactics also produced the desired buzz. Game on; a nation-wide movement was underway.

Derek Hess

Page 117: Born into an artistic family (his dad was the head of the Industrial Design department at the Cleveland Institute of Art), the young Derek Hess imagined tanks and airplanes in his head. When his father got home from work, Hess would elaborate on his conceptions, and his father would draw them for him. This experience eventually led to an art career. He graduated from the Center for Creative Studies in Detroit, majoring in printmaking. After college, Hess, heavily into music, booked bands for the Euclid Tavern and started to design and print the flyers. Soon he was producing posters for bands like Pink Floyd and Pearl Jam. His creations are now in the Rock and Roll Hall of Fame and the Louvre. Currently he creates almost no posters, focusing instead on pen-and-ink drawings, acrylic paintings, and screen prints.

Debra Campbell

Page 118: This is an unusual poster, since Obama has the globe in his mouth, but it is an interesting way to portray the idea of global unity. Debra Campbell created several open-edition Obama campaign posters.

Ray Noland

Page 119: One of Ray Noland's more popular offset, open-edition prints, this poster was also used on the road in various states and in the store on Gotellmama.org. Revenue from poster sales kept Ray rolling. Taking off in his 1997 Subaru, Noland's CRO (Creative Rescue Organization) hit the road to put up posters and hold Go Tell Mama! art shows in primary states like Texas, Pennsylvania, California, and North Carolina. Noland ended up at Manifest Hope in Denver and then struck out on the campaign trail throughout the general election. With the inauguration of Barack Obama on January 20, 2009, the dream became reality.

David Macaluso

Page 121: *Warrior Politics,* a signed-and-numbered limited-edition giclée print of 3,500, portrays a tough, determined candidate capable of the long haul. A special feature of David Macaluso's paintings is that he creates his own oil paints from recycled motor oil.

Eddie

Page 122: Here a tight-smiling Obama appears more beneficent. This is the only poster on which Eddie chose to use the color red.

Snuffhouse

Page 123: James Widener (a.k.a. Snuffhouse) is an illustrator and graphic artist heavily influenced by traditional street art. He grew up in the skateboarding and surf community of Florida and in Guatemala and says that "art and design came hand in hand with everything he loved doing." Paul Brody and Paul Rand got Widener interested in design and illustration at an early age. After graduating from Full Sail University with a degree in digital media, Widener has taken what he calls his "strange and bizarre renditions of human intent and combined it with animal emotion and his love of all things furry." In 2007, still in school, he started Snuffhouse, a design collective and a brand under which to work. Demonstrating a stubborn commitment to originality, Widener admits that he is fond of the work of Michael Sieben, Bruno 9li, Dalek, and Thomas Campbell.

Tim Hinton

Page 124: Tim Hinton has a reputation worldwide as a powerful African-American artist. His giclée print, entitled *Pride II*, was unveiled in a signed-and-numbered limited edition of fifty, and he also painted several stirring Obama portraits against the American flag. This self-taught artist grew up in Orlando, Florida, became a Marine, and was wounded twice in Vietnam, winning two Purple Hearts. The official poster for the signing of the Martin Luther King Holiday Legislation in 1983 was also created by Hinton. He enjoys teaching watercolor classes, rendering architecture, and illustrating children's books, and he maintains that he has the gift of taking ordinary moments and making them extraordinary. His work can be found in many museums and collections, including the Museum of African Art, the Smithsonian, the Kennedy Center, and the Frederick Douglass Home in Washington, D.C.

HVW8

Page 125: Tyler Gibney and Gene Pendon founded Heavyweight Production House, Inc. ("HVW8") in 1998 in Montreal, Canada. An eclectic co-op typical of the worldwide urban art movement, Heavyweight mixed 1970s funk, 1980s New York graffiti, comic book art, and retro LP album covers and brought together DJs, filmmakers, and assorted musicians. Openings included art hanging on the wall, art being done on the floor, comic jams, music, film, dancing—a party. In the 1990s they created "composition pieces" around famous people they dubbed heavyweights like Miles Davis, Richard Pryor, Noam Chomsky, and Mies van der Rohe. Working with old newspapers, photographs, pop iconography, sketches, etc., the artists then free-styled (like jazz) to produce a composition that honored the chosen individual. In 2003 HVW8 moved to Los Angeles. Enthused by Obama's candidacy, HVW8 produced a four-color, signed-and-numbered limited-edition screen print entitled *Hope / Change*.

Gabe Usadel

Page 126: Growing up in central Illinois, Gabe Usadel reports that he was surrounded by "music, art, and Midwestern love." As a child, he was heavily influenced by the pop culture that pervaded nearly everything: record album covers, *X-Men*, and *Star Wars*. In high school he discovered Miles Davis, Annie Liebowitz, Milton Glaser, Philippe Starck, and Pentagram. Graduating in graphic design from the University of Illinois, Usadel is presently the creative director of Ogilvy and Mather. His projects include work for the Steppenwolf Theatre, the Chicago 2016 Olympics, Oscar Mayer, and many other clients. His work has been recognized widely, and he has won a number of awards. His outstanding Obama poster design, which relies entirely on nonverbal communication, is a signed-and-numbered limited edition of fifty.

The Half and Half

Page 127: The Half and Half, Sarah Thomas and Nick Wilson, a male-female design team in Columbia, South Carolina, met in a design class at the University of South Carolina. She says she was impressed that there was another person interested in screen-printing. He says he really thought she had neat socks. They went into business together and screen-printed many a poster. Sharing an aesthetic makes working together easier, and each respects the design opinions of the other. Their Obama poster, in an edition of two hundred, relies totally on communication without words and is, amazingly, a collage of one-inch squares taken from over seventy comic book covers.

Deroy Peraza

Pages 128–130: Deroy Peraza's *The New Hope* was issued in a set of four colors and in signed-and-numbered editions of fifty. His later print, *We Made History*, was marketed through Hyperakt in a signed-and-numbered limited-edition screen print of one hundred in each of four colors to commemorate Barack Obama's election on November 4, 2008. The run sold out quickly, and very few copies have come up for resale due to Peraza's wonderful use of color stenciling. To celebrate the election, Peraza designed *Victory*, a set of six posters in a rainbow of colors, all in signed-and-numbered limited editions of one hundred.

Amy Martin

Page 131: Amy Martin's computer-designed *Hope* poster was a sensation the minute it was released. Having grown up in Michigan, she said she wanted to design a poster that appealed to Midwestern women. She accomplished her goal, and three thousand offset copies were mailed to members of the Democratic Women's Caucus. A signed-and-numbered limited giclée edition of two hundred was also printed by Heine-Weber of Santa Monica. Martin designed several other outstanding Obama posters, but for unknown reasons they only have digital lives. These include a poster with the *Hope* design, the wording "Change, a Change," and many more logo-winged butterflies, as well as an L.A. gig poster.

Alex Pardee

Page 132, *top left:* Alex Pardee split the signed-and-numbered, limited-edition screen print he did for Upper Playground by producing two runs of one hundred each in yellow/gray/black and pink/blue/red. Facial stenciling in pink/blue/red is very effective, especially with Obama's head raised, his eyes on the prize, and against a backdrop of the campaign's major themes (perhaps mantras) of hope, change, and progress.

Shepard Fairey

Page 132, *top right:* In February 2008, Shepard Fairey created the powerful poster *Hope* that successfully branded the Obama campaign, and the artist moved from popular California "outsider" to big-time outsider/insider by creating a number of different designs for the Obama campaign. We all know Shepard Fairey now, or we recognize his poster *Hope* and other Obama designs because they are everywhere—including as covers for *Time, Esquire, Smithsonian,* etc. After an arrest outside his Boston retrospective and a lawsuit with the Associated Press, one can anticipate a stunning series of posters from jail entitled: *From the Boston City Jail.*

The Mac

Page 132, b*ottom left:* The Mac's eye-catching poster *Hope* was an early entry in the burgeoning Obama poster/print movement. It was released in two slightly varied signed-and-numbered limited editions totaling two hundred prints for both editions. The print was out in time to see service in the critical Pennsylvania, Texas, and Ohio primaries, and this was the first poster distributed by Matt Revelli, founder of Upper Playground. A Southern California artist, the Mac heard Obama speak in Arizona and found himself "very optimistic about a candidate." The Mac wanted to portray Obama as "dignified, serious, and presidential," and he did so by using a red-stenciled, henna-like pattern on Obama's face. The artist got his start painting graffiti in the 1990s and credits Alfonse Mucha as an influence.

David Choe

Page 132, *bottom right:* Southern California fine artist David Choe created a painting entitled *Hope,* one of the most outstanding pieces of Obama campaign art. Also in the Upper Playground series, Choe's print, a signed-and-numbered limited-edition screen print of two hundred that sold out online within hours, has been widely seen as rivaling Shepard Fairey's iconic poster of the same name. Magazine covers for *Giant Robot* and *Ambassador* also widened his exposure. His wry sense of humor and a vocabulary dependent upon four-letter Anglo-Saxon derivatives create a funny, volatile mix. During the campaign, Choe and his brother James printed up some offset posters and set off in a van, pasting them up wherever and using them to create poster installations when possible. Choe's work was also a part of the Manifest Hope art shows in Denver and in Washington, D.C.

Sam Flores

Page 133, *top left:* Sam Flores, a New Mexico native, is enamored of mythological fantasy allegories, and he populates his paintings with costumed urchins and thin, beautiful women immersed in lush fields of flowers painted with warm color palettes reminiscent of turn-of-the-century art nouveau. Flores acknowledges influences from the great Czech painter and poster maker Alphonse Mucha as well as Michael Parker, Maurice Sendak (creator of *Where the Wild Things Are*), and poster maker Derek Hess. Moving beyond painting, Flores has furthered his reputation by creating skateboard and snowboard designs. A solo show in 2006, *Water under the Bridge,* featured a fifteen-foot-tall, sculpted Fatima doll dressed in a kimono atop a Japanese *koi* and a prodigious number of lovebirds. This is another Upper Playground print in a signed and numbered, limited-edition screen print of two hundred.

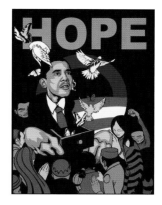

Alex Pardee

Page 133, *top right:* Alex Pardee's style reflects his experience as a graffiti artist and his love of horror movies, gangster rap, the Garbage Pail Kids, and the comic *Tales from the Crypt.* For years Pardee suffered long bouts of severe depression and posits that his art is therapy. Pardee began combining sketches and drawings—a world of bizarre monsters—into small books that he placed inside tattoo and porn magazines in waiting rooms and public restrooms around greater San Francisco. These caught on and were published in 1999. On political involvement, Pardee commented: "I am not normally one to get too political in my art, unless of course you look *very* deeply into some of my naked, four-armed, retarded beasts or my over-cross-hatched wrinkles. However, I am a huge Obama supporter, and I *jumped* at the chance to help out."

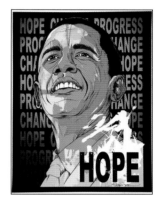

Franke

Page 133, *bottom left:* Franke was raised in Austria, Germany, and Spain. From the time he was young, he drew handmade comic books of his own creation. Bored in a German specialized design school, he left for Vienna, where he forged art and drew pornographic comics to make a living. His experiences on the street, with its vibrant underground of pinup magazines, tattoo shops, and what he calls low-brow art, all shaped in him a rebellious spirit. In Amsterdam he again lived life at the bottom, but while he was working in rock music clubs, he began to design album covers. Back in Vienna he set up shop and now operates a successful business producing graphic materials of a wide variety. His signed-and-numbered limited-edition giclée print of six hundred, *Hope,* was exhibited at the Manifest Hope show in Denver.

Cody Hudson

Page 133, *bottom right:* Growing up in Kenosha, Wisconsin, Cody Hudson worked at Pizza Popper and Piggly Wiggly and even painted animation cells for the cartoon *Sparky the Firedog.* After graduating from a two-year technical school, he got a job at a weekly coupon magazine working on an early Mac—the ones with the green screen. Hudson finally settled in Chicago. He likes to use simple, colorful shapes, and this preference is clearly expressed in his print *Hope,* which was one of the last in the Upper Playground series, a signed-and-numbered limited-edition screen print of fifty.

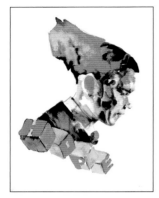

David Choe

Page 134: David Choe's second creation for Upper Playground was also a signed-and-numbered limited-edition screen print in a run of two hundred. Not as popular as Choe's more painterly *Hope* print, the colorful, tumbling-block treatment of the word "hope," coupled with the orange/yellow map attached to the back of Obama's head, creates an innovative, bold design. You judge.

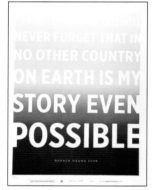

Morning Breath

Page 135: Doug Cunningham and Jason Noto began collaborating in 1996 in San Francisco, California, to dream up skateboard designs. Their designs appealed to the young skateboarder crowd, and their experience with graffiti art helped. In 2002 they traded the west coast for the east coast and started Morning Breath in Brooklyn, New York. Not limited to skateboard design, the partners produced music album designs and were nominated for a Grammy Award in 2004 for "best special music packaging." Cunningham and Noto, in their creative work, aim at a "balance of art, design, and advertising." That goal is well realized in the Obama poster the pair created that was sold through Upper Playground, a signed-and-numbered limited edition of two hundred screen prints that sold out online almost immediately.

Jonathan Hoefler

Page 136, *top left:* Jonathan Hoefler, an outstanding typeface designer, was also impressed with Obama's speeches and his respect for words and used snippets from those speeches to create this poster. In the *Artists for Obama* series, the print was sold online in a numbered edition of five thousand. Hoefler has designed award-winning typefaces for *Rolling Stone, Harper's Bazaar,* the *New York Times Magazine, Sports Illustrated,* and *Esquire.* Millions of Americans, most unknowingly, see Hoefler's work daily because he designed the typeface for the Mac operating system. The Obama campaign was sensitive to the importance of typeface and standardized all printed campaign materials in varieties of Gotham.

Jason H. Phillips

Page 136, *top right:* Ever since he was a child, Jason Phillips liked to draw and paint. He grew up in Detroit and graduated from Wayne State University, winning many art awards and scholarships along the way. He studied with nationally known painters Charles Parness and Janet Fish. Phillips founded Roots Visual Designs in 1996, and he has undertaken projects for McDonald's, Miller Genuine Draft, and Pelle Pelle Fashion. Enthused by Obama's candidacy, he created both a signed, open, offset-edition election poster and a signed, open-edition commemorative inauguration poster. Often focusing on life in the African-American community as a subject, Phillips says, "I want my work to make the viewer think about social issues or see a side of society that rarely gets documented in art."

Official Obama Campaign

Page 136, *bottom left:* Obama was hailed in Europe with a tremendous welcoming not seen since the arrival of Woodrow Wilson after World War I or since President Kennedy's speech before an anxious but enthused crowd in Germany's divided capital on June 26, 1962—"Ich bin ein Berliner." American presidents making important speeches in Berlin have become somewhat of a tradition. For another example, Ronald Reagan on June 12, 1987, stood before the Berlin Wall and challenged: "Mr. Gorbachev, tear down this wall." Obama attempted to win the hearts and minds of Berliners not just with rhetoric but with this wonderfully designed poster in the Bauhaus style. A controversy swirls around whether or not the poster was ever printed by the Obama campaign or was simply available as a free download to Berliners.

Official Obama Campaign

Page 136, *bottom right:* An official Obama campaign design, *Change,* was tailored to other states as well. What allowed the Obama campaign staff this kind of freedom was the tremendous amount of money the campaign spent on design—a poster designer's dream come true.

David Springmeyer

Page 137: Chicago-based David Springmeyer produced the *Grant Park* print electro-photographically at 600 dpi in a signed-and-numbered limited edition of one hundred. Additionally he produced a revised version of this print, as well as an Obama baseball-card-like print. He became interested in poster art while taking a course in screen-printing at the Lill Street Art Center. He prides himself on combining traditional textual and graphic elements with the latest digital editing techniques.

Justin Kemerling

Page 188: Justin Kemerling, situated in Lincoln, Nebraska, created two Obama prints and two *Vote* prints over the course of the campaign. All four prints are giclée, signed-and-numbered limited editions. His campaign prints are a part of his efforts to use his art to support community activism. He works closely with Lincoln activist groups and strongly believes it is necessary to pick a side and push the cause. Favorite topics include peace, social justice, climate change, sustainability, and student organizing. On a website named Power to the Poster, his graphic creations in support of various causes can be downloaded for free. Kemerling asks: "As a global citizen, what moves you?"

This Is Our Moment | Justin Kemerling | 19" x 25"